111 Genius Ways to Survive the Madness of Motherhood

Ariana Naebrich

Imprint

First Englisch Edition, February 2025
Copyright © 2025 Ariana Naebrich

All rights reserved.

Reproduction, even in part, is not permitted. This work, including its individual components, is protected by copyright. Any use without the permission of the publisher and the author is prohibited. This includes, in particular, electronic or other forms of reproduction, translation, distribution, and public accessibility.

INTRODUCTION

Welcome to the Club of Survival Experts – or as we like to call it: Mom Madness!

You did it! No, I don't mean tying your kid's shoes in under 20 minutes or avoiding a tantrum at the supermarket – I mean finding a book that truly gets you. Welcome to "111 Genius Ways to Survive the Madness of Motherhood," your new survival guide for the toughest job in the world: **being a mom.**

This book is different. It doesn't preach, offer perfect parenting advice, or make promises that can't be kept (sorry, the baby will still wake up at night). Instead, you'll find 111 ways to tackle everyday challenges with humor, sarcasm, and a healthy dose of irony. From "How to Survive Morning Chaos" to "What to Do When Your Kid Asks Where Babies Come From," this book has got you covered.

Some situations will feel like they've been plucked straight from your own life, while others might not fit your current stage of motherhood. Maybe you're navigating diapers and baby food, while others are tackling school-age drama. No worries! Stress is stress, and the tips here are flexible enough to work in any kind of chaos.

INTRODUCTION

Along the way, you'll find fun puzzles, recipes, and coloring pages – because life is serious enough as it is. Oh, and don't worry: the swear words in here are 100% kid-friendly. You can quietly think them to yourself while continuing to be the calm, collected rock your family depends on. Or something like that.

So grab a coffee (or a glass of wine – no judgment here), kick up your feet, and get ready to survive the madness of motherhood in style. This book is a little reminder that you are a hero, every single day. And when things don't go as planned – don't worry, we've got 111 ways to help you keep going.

1 Coffee is Mom Magic!
Your Liquid Hero in Times of Need

There are those days when it feels like the world is conspiring against you – the alarm clock rings, the kids are whining, and the day's to-do list already feels like a boulder on your chest. And then there's the coffee. Or, more specifically: the lack of coffee.

Coffee isn't just a beverage. No, it's your secret weapon, your liquid hero in times of need. That first sip from your cup is like a hug that gently whispers, "You've got this." Whether it's piping hot or reheated for the fifth time, it gives you the strength to power through the day. Coffee doesn't make the chaos any less chaotic, but it definitely makes you better equipped to handle it.

So grab your cup and take this moment. Even if someone's already yelling in the background about a "missing" toothbrush (which you'll inevitably find exactly where it always is). With coffee in hand, you're the hero who can handle it all – even when your phone dings and someone needs help finding their socks.

2 Champagne Breakfast!
Luxury for Stressed-Out Heroines

Sometimes the day starts, and you just know: it's going to be a wild one. The alarm clock rings, toothpaste chaos decorates your freshly washed shirt, and the to-do list is already piling dangerously high – all before you've had your first sip of coffee. Welcome to mom life!

But today, you're doing it differently. Today, you're treating yourself to a champagne breakfast. Yes, you heard that right. Take this moment for yourself. A glass of chilled champagne, fresh croissants, a dollop of jam – and most importantly: peace and quiet. This little luxury isn't an escape; it's a conscious choice. You're recharging your batteries before the day can drain every last ounce of your energy.

A champagne breakfast is like a superhero cape – sparkling, empowering, and giving you the feeling that you can conquer anything. Whether the kids are throwing tantrums, the dog is racing through the living room, or the fridge mysteriously empties itself, this little ritual helps you start the day like the heroine you are.

cheers!

3 The Yoga of Serenity!
The Annoyed Monkey Saves the Day

--- ♥ --- ♥ --- ♥ ---

There are those moments when the stress just becomes too much. The kids are fighting over who gets the green cup, while your phone is overflowing with "urgent" messages from the daycare group. Deep breaths? If only. But today, you're trying something new: the "Annoyed Monkey."

Sit cross-legged on the floor. Straighten your back as if you're the queen of chaos – because, let's face it, you are. Close your eyes and take a deep breath. As you exhale, extend both middle fingers – not aggressively, but completely relaxed. Let the energy of resistance flow through you. It's a silent statement to the world that no one notices, but it gives you exactly the calm you need right now.

The Annoyed Monkey isn't just a yoga pose; it's your new anti-stress weapon. It's quiet, discreet, and absolutely liberating – even if the chaos around you continues to rage on. And the best part? It works anywhere: in the kids' room, at the dinner table, or right in the middle of the supermarket.

4 The 5-Minute Break!
Your Secret to Inner Calm

The laundry is piling up like an unconquerable mountain, your child is loudly protesting because they'll only eat pasta that's been cooked for exactly 2.8 minutes, and your phone is pinging nonstop with birthday reminders and family group messages. The world is practically demanding that you do everything all at once. But stop! It's time for the 5-Minute Break.

Lean back, take a deep breath, and leave everything as it is. These five minutes are just for you. It's not an escape; it's a conscious decision. Whether you stare into space, take a sip of coffee, or meditatively unwrap that emergency chocolate bar from your secret stash – this short pause gives you back your sense of control.

The 5-Minute Break isn't just a lifeline in the chaos of everyday life; it's a reminder that the world won't end just because you take a moment for yourself. And in the end, you'll realize: with a clear head, that mountain of tasks often gets tackled faster than you thought.

5 The Magical Laundry Chair!
Your Invisible Helper

Do you know it? That chair in the bedroom that mysteriously attracts everything no one wants to put away? Jackets, pants, socks – it all ends up on this enigmatic piece of furniture. You could swear it grows overnight. But today, you're not seeing it as an enemy but as your ally.

The laundry chair isn't messy; it's efficient. It saves you time. Why put away every single piece of clothing when you can toss it all into the washing machine in one go? And if your child asks why the chair is always so full, just tell them it's playing "adult Tetris."

With this magical helper, you won't just outsmart the laundry pile – you'll learn to accept that not every day has to be perfect. And sometimes, that's a mom's true superpower: letting go and letting the chair do its thing.

6 Breakfast Art for Tired Moms

Sometimes mornings are so hectic you wonder if you'll even have time for breakfast. But don't worry – today, we're turning your toast into a little masterpiece. Because starting the day creatively makes everything feel a bit brighter – and your kids will think you're a "MasterChef" genius.

Recipe Idea: Funny Breakfast Faces

- One slice of whole-grain toast
- Cream cheese or peanut butter (your choice)
- Fruit for decoration (e.g., blueberries for eyes, banana slices for ears, and apple pieces for a smiling mouth)

Spread the toast with your chosen topping, decorate it with a funny face, and voilà: breakfast with a side of entertainment. And if it doesn't turn out as planned, just call it "abstract art" – that always works.

7 Sudoku for Mom's Break
Clearing Your Mind

Sometimes, you don't need words, noise, or a to-do list – just a little peace and a moment for yourself. That's where your personal Sudoku comes in, giving you the chance to clear your mind and step away from the everyday madness.

While the kids argue over who gets to color with the blue marker, grab a pen and dive into your puzzle. It's more than just a break – it's a workout for your patience. And in the end, you'll be the mom who not only solves everything but also finishes the Sudoku.

		9			8	1		
	4	5			2			3
1		2	3	7			6	
8	7					6		9
	6						3	
9		4					1	7
	1			6	9	3		2
4			1			5	8	
		6	4			7		

8 Coloring Page!
Step Away from the Stress

There are days when everything feels like too much – the kids are whining, the housework is calling, and you can't seem to find the light at the end of the tunnel. That's exactly when you need a break. And what's more relaxing than coloring? Grab some pencils and get started!

Coffee Time

As you fill the lines with color, you'll see not just a picture come to life, but also your stress melt away. And if the kids get curious and want to join in – even better. The chaos can wait five more minutes.

9 The Magical Laundry Challenge

Laundry piles. They're endless, unbeatable, and multiply faster than you can yell, **"Kids, bring your clothes downstairs!"** But today, we're doing it differently: we're turning laundry into a game – the Magical Laundry Challenge.

The Task:
Set a timer for 10 minutes and let the kids compete against you.

The Goal:
Who can fold the most clothes before the time runs out?

Bonus Points:
Award extra points for creatively folded socks and super-speedy pants stacks.

By the end, you'll either be amazed at how much gets done in 10 minutes or end up with a pile of crumpled clothes that makes you laugh out loud. And yes, even that counts as a win.

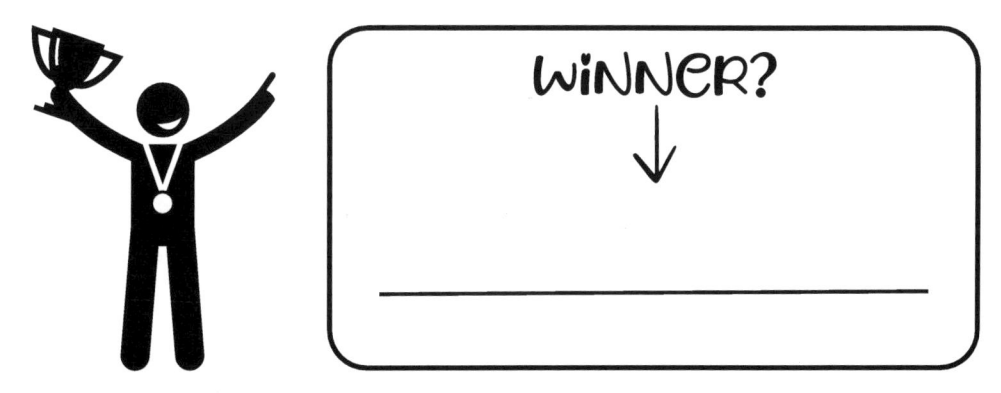

WINNER?
↓
_____

10 Would You Rather?
Mom Edition

Sometimes, you just need a break to laugh. Here comes "Would You Rather?" – the perfect mix of distraction and fun for moms.

Questions:

Would you rather face a traffic jam every time you drive to daycare or spend your days picking toys out of Lego pieces?

_____

Would you rather always drink cold coffee or never eat chocolate again?

_____

Would you rather help out at a birthday party with 15 kids or lead a parent-teacher meeting?

_____

Would you rather go without the internet for a week or watch your kids' favorite show for three hours every day?

_____

11 The Anti-Tidying Mantra
Chaos is Just a Phase

Sometimes you look around and think, "How did this happen? It was clean here yesterday!" And then you remember – you have kids. **Welcome to the chaos circus.** But instead of stressing out, try embracing the Anti-Tidying Mantra:

"It's okay if toys are everywhere."

"It's okay if the table looks like a craft store exploded."

"It's okay if the couch has been transformed into a fort of blankets and pillows."

And why? Because the chaos is proof that your kids are creative, happy, and active. Let the mess sit for a day and enjoy the moment. You can always clean up tomorrow – or just toss everything into a laundry basket and call it "tidying up."

12 Kids' Cookie Magic
A Recipe for Every Occasion

Sometimes everyone needs a break – mom, kids, and the chaos. What better way to unwind than baking together? Here's your super-easy recipe for magical happiness cookies.

Ingredients:

- 200 g flour
- 100 g sugar
- 100 g butter
- 1 egg
- 1 tsp vanilla sugar
- (Optional: chocolate chips or sprinkles)

Instructions:

1. Knead all ingredients into a smooth dough.
2. Let the kids cut out fun shapes. (Tip: Encourage creativity – dinosaur or star-shaped cookies are extra fun!)
3. Bake at 180°C (356°F) for about 10–12 minutes.
4. Enjoy – with coffee for you and cocoa for the little ones.

While the cookies are in the oven, you'll have a few minutes of peace – and the kids will be thrilled. A win-win!

13 City, Country, Chaos
The Family Game for In-Between Moments

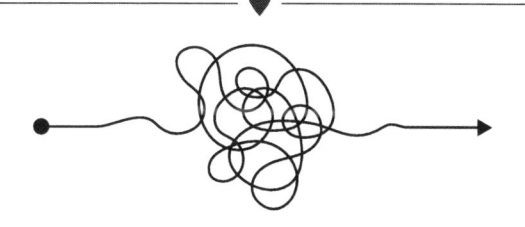

Sometimes you desperately need something to keep the kids busy – and yourself too. Enter the mom edition of "**City, Country, River.**"

How to Play:

1. Each family member writes down the categories: "City," "Country," and "Chaos."
2. Chaos is the special category – this is where you list things that only happen in your household (e.g., "**Thing Mom is always looking for**" or "**Phrase Dad always says**").
3. Pick a letter and get started!

Whoever comes up with the most creative answers wins. And even if no one feels like playing anymore, you've at least gained a few minutes of peace while everyone was thinking.

14 AN EMERGENCY CURSE WORD
The Secret Weapon of Mom Pros

There are moments when you just want to throw it all – the laundry pile, your phone, and maybe even your patience.

That's exactly why you need a secret curse word. Something only you know, something you can say in your head without offending the little ears around you.

An example? "Blabberpickle!" or "Blockhead Baron!"

The beauty of it? It relieves your stress and often makes you laugh because it sounds so ridiculous. Give it a try. The right curse word can work wonders – and no one needs to know why Mom is suddenly muttering to herself.

15 The Invisible Playground
Create Adventures at Home

Sometimes the playground is too far, the motivation too low, or the weather too bad. No problem! Today, the living room transforms into an adventure zone.

Ideas for the Invisible Playground:

- **Deluxe Pillow Fight**: Stack pillows and blankets to create obstacle courses or build a fortress.

- **Treasure Hunt**: Hide small surprises around the room and let the kids become explorers on a discovery mission.

- **Balloons Instead of Balls**: A few inflated balloons can turn even the dullest living room into a playland.

While the kids let off steam, you can sneak in a quiet moment – or join in and show off your supermom powers.

16 Mom Sudoku
A Quick Puzzle for In-Between Moments

--- ♥ --- ♥ --- ♥ ---

Some days, even the tiniest bit of peace feels like pure gold. That's exactly what this Sudoku is for. Take five minutes for yourself, grab a pen, and dive into the world of numbers. If you solve it, you'll feel like a genius – and if not, it was still a fantastic excuse to escape for a moment.

6	1		9		5	2		
8		9	2		7	1		
2								
5			7				9	6
	9	8	4		6	3	2	
3	7				2			1
								3
		3	5			8	9	4
		5	3		9		7	2

17 Family Movie Night
Popcorn and Pajamas

Sometimes, you don't need a big outing to make an evening magical. Turn your living room into a family cinema and enjoy a movie night that will be a highlight for everyone.

Here's How:

- Slip into cozy pajamas – family dress code is mandatory!
- Make fresh popcorn (recipe below).
- Pick a movie everyone loves (or invoke the "Mom decides" rule).

Popcorn Recipe:

- 3 tbsp oil
- 100 g popcorn kernels
- 2 tbsp sugar (for sweet popcorn) or a pinch of salt (for savory popcorn)

Heat the oil in a pot, add the popcorn kernels, and cover it with a lid. Shake the pot occasionally until the popping stops. Then season to your liking and enjoy!

By the end of the night, you'll have watched a great movie and created a memory that will outlast any to-do list.

JUST BREATHE

The Worst Words That Cross My Mind (But I Never Say Out Loud)

- [ ] _____
- [ ] _____
- [ ] _____
- [ ] _____
- [ ] _____
- [ ] _____
- [ ] _____
- [ ] _____
- [ ] _____
- [ ] _____
- [ ] _____

BRAT

18 Your Mini Escape
The Bathroom Paradise

The bathroom isn't just for brushing your teeth – it's your secret retreat. When the chaos in the house becomes too much, declare it a mom-only zone and indulge in a little wellness escape.

Your Ritual:

- Fill the bathtub with hot water and your favorite bubble bath (optional: add a handful of sea salt for extra relaxation).
- Dim the lights or light a candle – you deserve the full spa experience.
- Grab a book or listen to your favorite music – the kind that doesn't include kids' songs.

And if the kids come knocking? Just imagine you're on a tropical island and ignore them. This time is yours. Ten minutes of pure peace can work wonders to recharge your mom batteries.

19 The Magical Fridge
What Should I Cook Today?

There are those evenings when you stare into the fridge and feel like it just can't keep up with your chaos. The kids are complaining, your partner's asking what's for dinner, and you're thinking, **"Why not pizza made of air and love?"**

Here's your solution: The Magical Fridge Trick. Take a look at what you have and whip up a quick "Leftover Deluxe" meal. **Some ideas:**

- Pasta with whatever the fridge has to offer.
- DIY wraps – everyone makes their own, saving you from endless debates.
- Breakfast for dinner: pancakes or scrambled eggs always work.

The best part about this method? You can ditch the stress by selling it as a "culinary adventure." What matters isn't the perfect dinner, but that everyone leaves the table full and happy.

20 The Secret Emergency Chocolate Bar

TOP SECRET

Sometimes, enough is enough. It's one of those days when the kids are bouncing off the walls, the dog won't stop barking, and you're wondering why no one ever puts their shoes away, even though they're always in the way. That's when you need your secret emergency chocolate bar.

This isn't just any snack – it's your lifeline, your moment of peace. Hide it somewhere only you know (like behind the cleaning supplies – no one's ever looking there).

When the world feels like too much, indulge in this little bit of chocolate therapy.

And the best part? No guilt. This bar isn't a weakness – it's a smart strategy to recharge your supermom powers.

Sometimes, all it takes is one little bite to find the energy to take on the rest of the day.

21 Family Bingo
Chaos, But With Structure

Some days, family life feels like an endless whirlwind of tasks, questions, and arguments. That's where Family Bingo comes in – a game that turns chaos into fun and keeps everyone entertained.

How It Works:

1. Create a bingo card with squares like:
    - "Someone lost a sock."
    - "A glass of water was spilled."
    - "Mom shouts: 'Pick that up!'"
    - "The baby spit up."
    - "The cat is sitting on the table."
2. Everyone gets a card, and as events happen, they mark them off. The first person to complete a row wins!

The Prize:

A hug, a cookie, or the right to choose the next family movie. And even if no one wins, you've still found a reason to laugh in the middle of the madness

22 The Power of the Power Nap!

Some days, coffee just isn't enough. Your energy hits rock bottom, and even the simplest tasks feel like mountains. That's when it's time to bring out your secret weapon: THE **POWER NAP**.

Lie down for 15 to 20 minutes. That's all it takes to recharge your batteries. Put your phone on silent, ignore the to-do list, and give yourself this moment.

Yes, the world will keep spinning, and the chaos will still be there – but you'll be better equipped to handle it afterward.

And if the kids come knocking, just tell them that Mom is recharging her superpowers. If you're lucky, they'll be so curious they might actually leave you alone.

23 The Lego Challenge
Build Yourself a Break

Lego bricks – both a blessing and a curse. But today, we're turning them into your everyday hero! The Lego Challenge is the perfect activity for kids: it sparks creativity and gives you a few precious moments to relax.

Here's How:

- Give the kids a challenge: "Build the tallest Lego tower you can!" or "Create a Lego bridge that can hold a stuffed animal."
- For older kids, set a time limit or assign creative themes like "A Dinosaur Lego Zoo."

While the little builders are hard at work, you can enjoy a moment of peace – or join in and show them that Mom still has the best Lego skills.

And the best part? By the end, you'll have not just a masterpiece but also a reminder that Lego is so much more than just a tripping hazard in your daily life.

YOUR
DIARY
MOMENT

Dear Diary...

DATE: _____

24 The Magical Lipstick Ritual

Sometimes you feel completely drained, like a phone at 5% battery with no charger in sight. That's when the magical lipstick ritual comes to the rescue – a simple trick to make you feel like the superhero you are in just seconds.

Grab your favorite lipstick and put it on, even if you're just standing in the kitchen. It's not about looking perfect; it's about giving yourself the confidence to tackle anything – whether it's a child's tantrum or the mountain of spaghetti after dinner.

And if anyone asks why you're all dolled up, just say: **"For me. I've got a date with chaos today – and I'm going to win."**

25 Deluxe Blanket Fort Adventures in the Living Room

A few blankets, a few pillows – and suddenly, your living room transforms into a magical fortress that would amaze even the greatest adventurers.

How to Build Your Blanket Fort:

1. Drape blankets between sofas, chairs, and tables to create a sturdy fort structure.
2. Use pillows for interior padding to make the fort extra cozy.
3. Add battery-operated fairy lights or flashlights to set the perfect mood.

Once the fort is built, the adventure begins: read thrilling stories, play knights and princesses, or simply enjoy a little break in the safety of the blankets.

For the kids, it's an adventure – for you, it's a much-needed escape from the daily grind.

little
ADVENTURER

26 The Morning Luxury Coffee
A Ritual Just for You

Before the day with all its demands comes crashing down on you, take a moment just for yourself – with your morning coffee as the star of the show.

It's not just about the taste; it's about the ritual of giving yourself a small pause before the chaos begins.

Sit in your favorite spot, hold that first steaming cup of the day, and take a deep breath. Let the world wait while you savor your coffee.

Whether the kids are already loudly demanding breakfast or your mental to-do list is screaming at you, this little moment is yours and yours alone.

And if the coffee goes cold? Just reheat it. It's not a sign of defeat – it's a statement: **"I deserve this moment."**

27 The Living Room Concert
Rockstars of Everyday Life

Sometimes the best way to release built-up energy is to let it all out – with music! Turn your living room into a concert stage and let the kids (and yourself) become stars.

Here's How:

- Pick a playlist with your favorite songs. Whether it's kids' hits, classics, or your personal power anthems – anything goes.
- Hand out "instruments": pots and wooden spoons for drums, hairbrushes for microphones, and anyone who wants can just dance wildly.
- Let the kids perform, and cheer them on like their number-one fan.

And if you feel like letting loose, grab a hairbrush and rock the stage yourself. It doesn't matter how it sounds – what matters is the fun. By the end, everyone will be happy and (hopefully) a little tired.

28 Calm in the Chaos
The 3-MIN Meditation

Between piles of laundry, endless kid questions, and a to-do list that seems to grow on its own, there's often no time for a long break. But three minutes? You can always spare those – with a quick meditation.

Here's How:

1. Find a quiet spot (even a locked bathroom door will do in a pinch).
2. Close your eyes and focus on your breath. Inhale deeply and exhale slowly.
3. Repeat a mantra in your mind, like: "I've got this" or "The chaos can wait; I'm in control."

In just three minutes, you'll feel clearer, more focused, and ready to face the day again. The world keeps spinning, but you've pressed pause – and that's enough to recharge.

29 The Creative Kitchen
Cooking as Family Art

Sometimes the kitchen is the best place to bring everyone together – not just for eating, but for creating something special as a team. Today, you're not just cooking; you're making magic!

Here's How:

1. Let the kids help create a simple dish, like homemade pizza.
2. Set up: Provide various ingredients such as dough, tomato sauce, cheese, veggies, and anything else you love.
3. Everyone decorates their own pizza and gives it a name ("Rocket Pizza," "Princess Margherita," etc.).

While the pizzas bake, you can laugh about the wildest ingredient combos or set the table together. In the end, it's not just about the food – it's about the feeling of togetherness, and that makes every meal better.

30 Decluttering for the Soul
The Closet of Forgotten Things

We all have those corners of the house we'd rather ignore – the drawer full of cables, the cabinet stuffed with old kids' drawings, or the overflowing shoe rack.

But today, it's time for a change. Time for some **"therapeutic decluttering."** Take 15 minutes and focus on just one area or one closet.

Go through each item and decide: keep, donate, or toss? Take a "before" photo of the chaos and an "after" photo when you're done – the transformation will feel priceless!

Decluttering feels like shedding extra weight – not just in your home, but in your mind. And if it's not perfect? That's okay. The closet of forgotten things can keep a few secrets for another day.

31 Family Quiz
Who Knows Mom Best?

Sometimes the kids (and the rest of the family) forget that Mom is more than just the organizer of chaos.

Time for a quiz that reminds them how amazing you are – and tests how well they really know you.

Ask a few fun questions about yourself, like "What is Mom's favorite food?", "How old was Mom when she learned to ride a bike?", or "What is Mom's favorite movie?". Let each family member share their answers, either on paper or out loud. The person with the most points gets to choose what's for dinner, of course within Mom-approved limits.

This quiz isn't just fun; it also shows everyone that Mom is a real person with her own likes, dreams, and quirks – not just the one who finds the missing socks.

Dinner Wish

_____

32 The Invisible Book Club
Just You, Your Book, and Peace

Sometimes, all you need is a moment to yourself – no kids, no to-do lists, no chaos. Your best ally? A book and a secret retreat.

It could be the storage closet, the car, or a comfy chair conveniently out of sight.

With your favorite book in hand and a few stolen minutes, you can forget the world. Tell the kids you're on a "mission," and let your partner take over for a while. Because in these moments, you're not really disappearing – you're recharging.

And when you emerge from your reading hideaway, you'll be ready to face the day with a smile once again.

Completed On: ☑

_____

Book Read:

_____

33 Your Show, Your Rules
The Evening Is Yours

When the kids are finally in bed and the house is somewhat quiet, the best moment of the day begins: show time.

Whether you're diving into a drama, laughing at a comedy, or unraveling the hundredth true-crime case, this is your time to unwind and forget the world.

Slip into your coziest clothes, curl up on the couch, and grab a blanket. Add a glass of wine or your favorite chocolate, and the evening is complete. **Most importantly: the remote is yours – tonight, no one else decides what's on**.

This little luxury reminds you that you're not just a mom, but also your own person – with your own preferences and a well-deserved break.

34 Sweet Escape
A Slice of Cake for the Soul

Sometimes all you need is a little slice of happiness – in the form of cake. The smell of freshly baked dough, the warmth from the oven, and that first bite can work wonders when life feels overwhelming.

Recipe for a Quick Happiness Cake:

- 200 g flour
- 150 g sugar
- 100 g butter (melted)
- 2 eggs
- 1 tsp baking powder
- 100 ml milk
- Optional: chocolate chips, nuts, or berries

Instructions:

1. Preheat the oven to 180°C (356°F).
2. Combine all the ingredients in a bowl and mix into a smooth batter.
3. Pour the batter into a greased baking pan and bake for about 30 minutes.
4. Let it cool, dust with powdered sugar, and enjoy – ideally with a cup of coffee or tea.

Take the time to bake this cake and savor it mindfully. Because sometimes, a sweet moment is all it takes to make the world feel a little brighter.

35 Sudoku Break
Numbers for the Soul

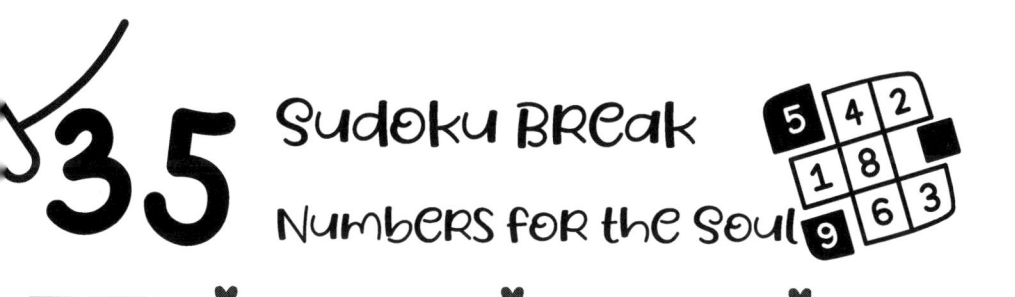

Sometimes your mind just needs a break from constant questions like "Where are my socks?" or "What's for dinner?". That's exactly what this Sudoku break is for. It's like a mini workout for your brain – only more relaxing.

Grab a pen, get comfortable, and dive into the puzzle. It's not just a moment of peace, but also a great way to clear your thoughts. And if the kids get curious, let them join in – a little teamwork (or cheating) on a Sudoku is perfectly fine too.

	7		2			9	6	
		4		9		7		
	1			6		8		4
	5	6		7		1		
2		1	5		6	4		9
		3		1		2	5	
1		2		5			8	
		7		8		6		
	3	8			7		4	

JUST BREATHE

The Best Excuses for "Mom Needs a Break":

- "I'm currently on a secret mission to find the perfect cup of coffee."
- "I'm conducting very important research on sleep deprivation."
- "I'm enjoying the absolute peace that only the bathroom can provide."
- "I'm taking a yoga break (except I'm just lying on the couch)."
- "I'm on a journey of self-discovery – please do not disturb."
- "I'm taking a nap – while standing, but please don't talk to me."

Space for Your Own Excuses:

- [ ] _____
- [ ] _____
- [ ] _____
- [ ] _____
- [ ] _____

KISS MY ASS!

36 Color and Unwind
Your Creative Moment

Sometimes, the best thing you can do is let your thoughts drift and let your pencil glide across the paper. A coloring page can work wonders to relieve stress and bring a little creativity into your day.

37 Word Search Fun
Words for Mom Life

A moment of calm paired with a little mental challenge – that's exactly what our word search puzzle offers. The words are taken straight from your daily life and couldn't be more fitting.

D	L	Z	Q	E	N	K	D	D	H	Z	E	Q	S	N	Q	S	B	X	S
W	Q	M	E	G	D	M	L	R	B	L	V	Q	L	I	A	L	R	B	I
T	Y	P	L	L	N	U	N	J	B	C	P	P	W	E	L	E	W	G	T
S	E	B	O	S	M	F	B	I	G	C	R	F	B	X	E	P	K	U
L	Z	S	V	M	S	S	E	R	T	S	W	E	B	X	V	P	B	M	R
S	N	Y	R	D	N	U	A	L	T	L	Q	N	D	J	Q	K	R	P	H
N	I	R	B	Y	B	Y	N	U	T	E	A	N	T	R	T	V	T	H	Z
J	F	R	I	C	L	L	D	R	Y	O	V	I	W	J	Z	B	G	E	A
G	X	M	A	K	B	K	O	J	A	V	U	D	B	O	Z	Y	B	U	P
T	Z	T	D	M	T	C	O	Q	K	F	P	H	F	D	C	Y	Z	H	X
H	E	A	V	F	J	K	G	G	K	H	O	H	Q	B	G	G	Y	B	Y
E	D	Y	E	O	I	K	I	Y	N	R	T	S	I	L	Y	A	K	Q	Y
R	A	U	N	N	S	Y	Z	D	I	W	A	M	X	J	J	U	X	V	T
E	Z	Z	T	E	I	J	F	R	B	A	Z	Y	L	A	K	V	K	Z	J
T	A	M	U	G	V	H	V	B	D	L	X	R	H	D	P	N	F	X	B
H	J	A	R	X	N	J	N	G	O	A	T	L	A	G	P	E	S	R	N
G	C	O	E	H	L	C	G	W	V	F	B	W	B	C	F	L	E	U	T
U	Q	Y	H	H	U	O	E	I	E	F	J	D	C	K	Y	A	T	L	D
A	D	H	N	V	A	V	E	W	Y	X	Y	C	G	Q	K	I	P	O	J
L	Y	Z	U	L	O	A	F	K	T	E	P	B	T	U	Q	E	X	F	M

ADVENTURE   BREAK   DINNER
GOAL   LAUGHTER   LAUNDRY
SLEEP   SOFA   STRESS

38 The Relaxing Bath
Just Dive In

There's hardly anything as soothing as a warm bath after a long day. When life gets chaotic, **the bathtub becomes your personal spa – and you've earned it**.

Run warm water, add a few drops of your favorite bath oil or bubbles, and dim the lights. Maybe light a candle or play your favorite music. As the water washes away your tension, close your eyes and think of absolutely nothing – or maybe the chocolate bar waiting for you afterward.

This moment is all yours. Tell your family you're on an important mission – and keep the door shut. Ten minutes of pure peace can work wonders.

39 Mini Bakery
Cookies for the Heart and Soul

Baking isn't just a treat for the taste buds – it's also a wonderful way to clear your mind. Today, you'll transform your kitchen into a mini bakery, creating cookies that bring joy to both you and the kids.

Recipe for Easy Butter Cookies:

- 250 g flour
- 125 g butter (cold and cubed)
- 100 g sugar
- 1 egg
- 1 tsp vanilla sugar

Instructions:

1. Combine all ingredients in a bowl and knead into a smooth dough.
2. Let the dough rest in the refrigerator for 30 minutes.
3. Roll it out on a floured surface and cut out fun shapes.
4. Bake at 180°C (356°F, top/bottom heat) for about 10–12 minutes.
5. Once cooled, decorate (e.g., with icing and sprinkles).

The best part? While the cookies bake in the oven, you can sit down and enjoy the wonderful aroma filling your kitchen.

40 The Chocolate Break Rule
Sweet Indulgence Without Compromise

Sometimes the best thing you can do for yourself is simply enjoy a piece of chocolate. No excuses, no special occasion – just the understanding that you deserve it.

Keep your chocolate stash hidden in a secret spot only you know (**like behind the veggie drawer in the fridge – no one will ever look there**). When the day gets particularly stressful, treat yourself to a piece or two. It's amazing what a little sweetness can do for your soul.

And if someone asks why Mom looks so happy? That's your little secret.

41 Stretch it out!
Quick Yoga for Any Moment

Everyday life is full of little stressors – the perfect opportunity to reset with a few simple yoga exercises. No mat or quiet room needed. All that matters is taking a moment for yourself.

Stand up straight, close your eyes briefly, and take a deep breath.

As you exhale, let your shoulders drop and relax your neck. Slowly stretch your arms above your head, then bend forward and let your hands reach for the floor – or as far as you can comfortably go.

Pause for a moment, take a few deep breaths, and then straighten back up.

The best part? This quick exercise fits anywhere – between piles of laundry, kids' questions, or while the pasta is boiling.

Just a few minutes are enough to stretch your body and clear your mind.

Namaste

42 Your Favorite Playlist
Music That Makes Everything Better

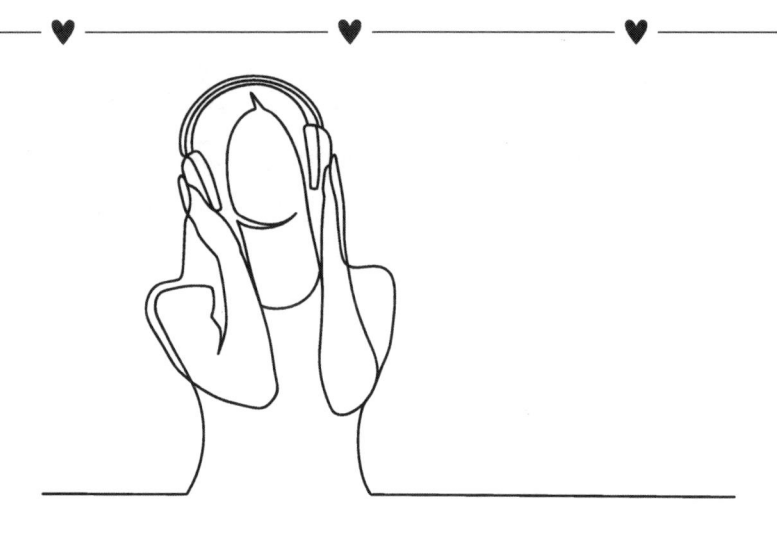

♥ ——— ♥ ——— ♥

Sometimes, the right song is all you need to recharge. Your favorite playlist isn't just a collection of songs – it's your secret weapon against daily stress.

Create a playlist with tracks that motivate, calm, or simply make you happy. Put on your headphones (or crank up the speakers if no one's complaining) and let the music transport you to another world. Whether you're cooking, tidying up, or just taking a break, music makes everything easier.

And if you're really in the mood? Dance like no one's watching – even if the kids are standing in the doorway laughing. It's these little moments that brighten the everyday.

43 The Spontaneous Walk
Fresh Air for New Energy

Sometimes the best way to clear your mind is to simply step outside – no matter the weather.

A short walk works wonders, whether you're alone or with the kids.

Put on your comfiest shoes, grab a scarf (or sunglasses, depending on the season), and let the fresh air put a stop to your spinning thoughts.

If you're walking alone, enjoy a few moments of complete silence or listen to a podcast that inspires you.

Walks don't have to be long to make an impact. Even a quick loop around the block can refresh you and give you the energy to tackle the day – whether it's for your responsibilities or just for yourself.

TOP SECRET

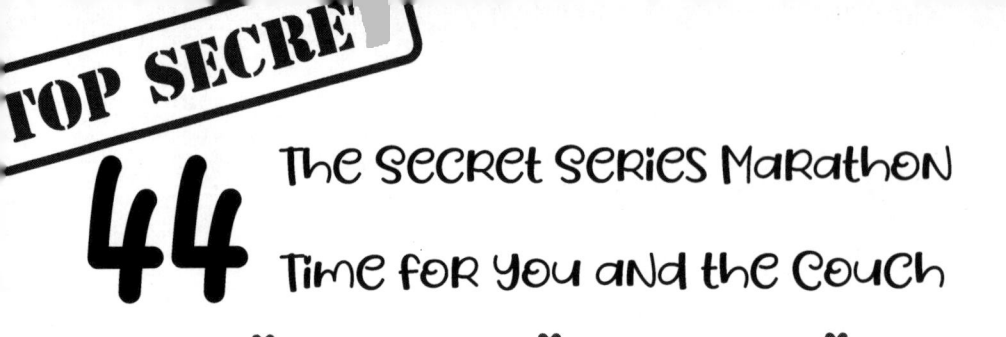

44 — The Secret Series Marathon
Time for You and the Couch

Sometimes all you need is yourself, your couch, and a series you've been dying to watch. No kids' songs, no documentaries about construction vehicles – today is Mom time.

Put your feet up, grab your favorite blanket, and start the series that's been sitting on your watchlist forever. Pair it with some snacks or a glass of wine, and let the world wait outside for a while.

It's not about how many episodes you get through – it's about the feeling of treating yourself to something that's just for you. And if anyone asks why Mom looks so happy on the couch? Just say: "It's my professional development in relaxation."

- ☑ Series
- ☑ Snacks
- ☑ Wine/Tea

45 The Kids' Kitchen
Little Chefs at Work

Sometimes, kids need an activity that not only keeps them busy but also brings them joy – and that's where the kids' kitchen comes in.

Let the little ones prepare their own meal while you relax as their coach (or audience).

Whether it's fruit skewers, open-faced sandwiches, or a simple yogurt with toppings – the possibilities are endless.

Give them the freedom to be creative and enjoy watching how proud they are of their creations. And if things get a bit messy? No problem – the smiles of your little chefs make it all worthwhile.

In the end, you'll not only have a mini feast but also a wonderful memory of a shared moment in the kitchen.

46 The Candle Ritual
Relaxation at Your Fingertips

There's nothing more soothing than the gentle flicker of a candle. When life feels overwhelming, create your own little retreat with a simple candle ritual.

Light your favorite candle, sit in a quiet spot, and take a few moments to watch the flame dance. Breathe deeply in and out, feel the warmth, and let your thoughts come and go.

Enhance the moment with a warm cup of tea or your favorite essential oil wafting through the room.

This small, peaceful moment just for you will give you the strength to face daily life with calm and clarity.

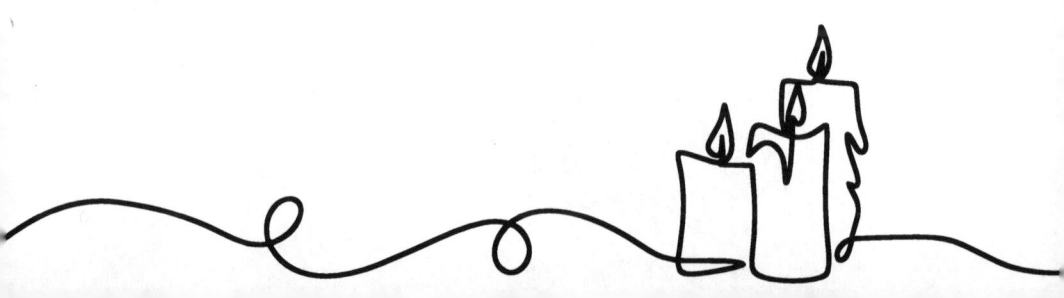

47 Word Salad Deluxe
A Puzzle for All Thinkers

Sometimes, a little mental challenge is exactly what you need to clear your mind. Here's your personal "Word Salad Deluxe" – a word search puzzle that's not only fun but also brings a touch of calm to your day.

```
X E P L E C V I U G I U A Y O R E S M K
W G I P Y E M J X F D K O P K L T F L F
P U A H Q L M Z M O M X C W C W W I R C
Z N W N Y Q I Z M R S S G A A P U Z S P
P S R T N X T D O O W V R I H F S K U O
B R S L U I E Z D B F I O V Y K H N Z A
Z J J K C Y V Z A B M G E L O V P U M S
F A R E T T D E W P V A J O Z J X Q J I
K Y W Q U N U K R L H Y B O V O Q R V U
J J H I S U B M S S Q U L N O Y Q J M W
T J E Z A I Q I X Y A B I G S M M G Y L
K E C J P A J B C Q J R R L Y P T X E Z
G S T U G F R C C D S V Y U K F E Q P T
R P I D L Z X G E E L F X J V J U F W I
F E C L V L B H L E K A O M J M O I N E
V M X U K V R D H A P F F R C M H Y H J
F N F O G B D M P F V E Y W T B Z X H L
O D J J N U O A L L I U E F W F H I O S
P H R R C L L A D P F Z Z Y D W T K J U
S N O I T S E U Q E U N W Y R H B B Y E
```

ANNIVERSARY	BOOKS	CUDDLES
FORT	HECTIC	JOY
MIRACLE	MOM	QUESTIONS

48 The Foot Bath Miracle
Quick Wellness for Any Moment

Sometimes, all it takes is a few minutes of self-care to turn your day around. **A foot bath is the perfect mini wellness retreat that's quick and easy to set up.**

Fill a large bowl or bucket with warm water, add a few drops of essential oil (like lavender or peppermint) or some bath salts, and immerse your feet.

As the water melts away the tension from your body, take a moment to relax – perhaps with a book or a small piece of chocolate.

After 10 minutes, you'll feel refreshed and renewed. The best part? It costs you almost no time, but the relaxation is priceless.

49 Start Your Day With Power
The Morning Routine of Champions

A great day begins with a powerful start – and a morning routine that's all about you. Before the kids wake up and the chaos begins, take a few minutes just for yourself.

Set your alarm 15 minutes earlier and use the time to do something that empowers you: a few yoga stretches, a peaceful cup of coffee, or some quick journaling. Write down three things you're grateful for or what you hope to accomplish that day.

This small moment in the morning gives you the calm and energy to take on the day. And if something disrupts your routine? No worries – it's the intention that counts, and you can always try again tomorrow.

GRATITUDE JOURNAL

S M T W T F S   DATE

TODAY, I AM GRATEFUL FOR

1.

2.

3.

SCHEDULE

-
-
-
-
-
-

DAILY AFFIRMATION

NOTES:

I AM PROUD OF

-
-
-

GRATITUDE JOURNAL

S   M   T   W   T   F   S   DATE

TODAY, I AM GRATEFUL FOR

1.

2.

3.

SCHEDULE

- ☐
- ☐
- ☐
- ☐
- ☐
- ☐

DAILY AFFIRMATION

NOTES:

I AM PROUD OF

○

○

○

50 The Happy Dance
Movement for the Soul

Sometimes, nothing beats stress like a little movement – and what's more fun than an impromptu dance? Whether you're dancing alone or with the kids, the **Happy Dance** is guaranteed to lift your spirits.

Turn on your favorite music, crank up the volume a little, and just start moving. No rules, no choreography – just you and the music. Let the kids invent their own moves, or come up with silly dances together.

After just a few minutes, you'll feel lighter, more energized, and a little freer – exactly what you need to carry on your day with a smile.

51 Number Magic
A Sudoku for Mom's Break

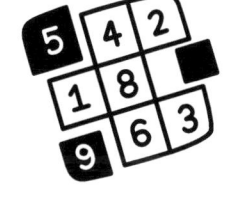

Sometimes, you just need a moment to focus on something small – and a Sudoku is perfect for that. It's a little mental challenge that lets you tune out the chaos of everyday life, even if just for a while.

				2	5			9
6					1	5		
4	8			9	6	3		
	4	8		5				3
7		2	4		3	8		1
5				8		9	2	
		3	2	7			4	5
		7	6					8
2			5	3				

52 Spa Feeling at Home
The 5-Minute Face Mask

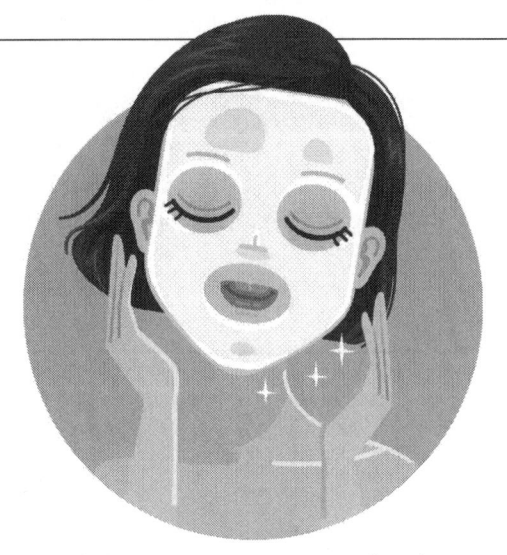

You don't need an elaborate setup to feel pampered – a face mask is all it takes. It's the quickest and easiest way to treat yourself while bringing a mini spa moment into your daily routine.

Grab your favorite mask (homemade or store-bought), apply it, and enjoy the short time while it works its magic.

Sit down, take a deep breath, and tune everything else out for those five minutes. Afterward, you'll not only feel refreshed but also a little more like the queen you truly are.

53 Vocabulary Madness
A Word Search Puzzle for You

Sometimes, a little puzzle fun is just what you need to escape the everyday chaos for a moment. Our word search puzzle is perfect for that – relaxing, entertaining, and just right for a well-deserved mom break.

```
Y Q F F G B N I X O S X W S I H L Z D E
U W F Z X L C B D W E H U S D V A K H D
D N D Q F Y D L C U V T O N K Z W D Z B
C H M A T H R D C B C B G W K X K B L X
O C M L X U I E X H R E G X E T R N H T
G O D E T J H T V E Y T E J K W P E L Q
T Y A A A V A U A O N I W R O G K L C B
N A D M B D F K E B C R V M N T W W F Y
O L Q D L J F L J A L E J U K I T G G I
B P A D E A W P O R O L R C U X T H J C
S O Q P S M X L L O J Q N V W Z R Q J Q
O N B T U L R Y X R R V J P B Z X E D U
A Q C U G B W L Q H E L P U X Y W E O B
H A O Q C O N F U S I O N S L U H I W W
C N M N Z R Y M Y Z G G O O N B B F E K
J L E K B T P Y P D D T Q G E N I I X I
U P L Q V W F Y E Q J I U U E R P U T S
Z T D F S P P A Q Y C N N C P H L A L G
Q K R V R Y P M D Y I I N J X J C V D M
K X R E T X O O L R X Y X O A M G Y D S
```

BREAKFAST	CHAOS	CONFUSION
DAD	FLOOR	HELP
PLAY	RECOVERY	TABLE

54 The Relaxing Hot Chocolate

There's nothing more comforting than a cup of hot chocolate. After a long day, it becomes your liquid moment of bliss – sweet, warm, and exactly what you need.

Recipe for the Perfect Hot Chocolate:

- 250 ml milk
- 2 tbsp cocoa powder (unsweetened)
- 1 tbsp sugar (or more, to taste)
- 50 g dark chocolate (chopped)
- A pinch of cinnamon or vanilla (optional)

Instructions:

1. Heat the milk in a small pot without bringing it to a boil.
2. Stir in the cocoa powder and sugar until dissolved.
3. Add the chopped chocolate and stir until fully melted.
4. Pour the hot chocolate into a mug and enhance with cinnamon or vanilla if desired.

Sit back, take a sip, and let the stress of the day fade away. Sometimes, a single cup is all it takes to set the world right again.

55 The Creative Break
Paint Like an Artist

When was the last time you painted something just for yourself? Today is the perfect day to do it. Grab some paper and pens or paints and create whatever comes to mind – a simple pattern, a flower, or a wild jumble of colors. This isn't about perfection; it's about letting go.

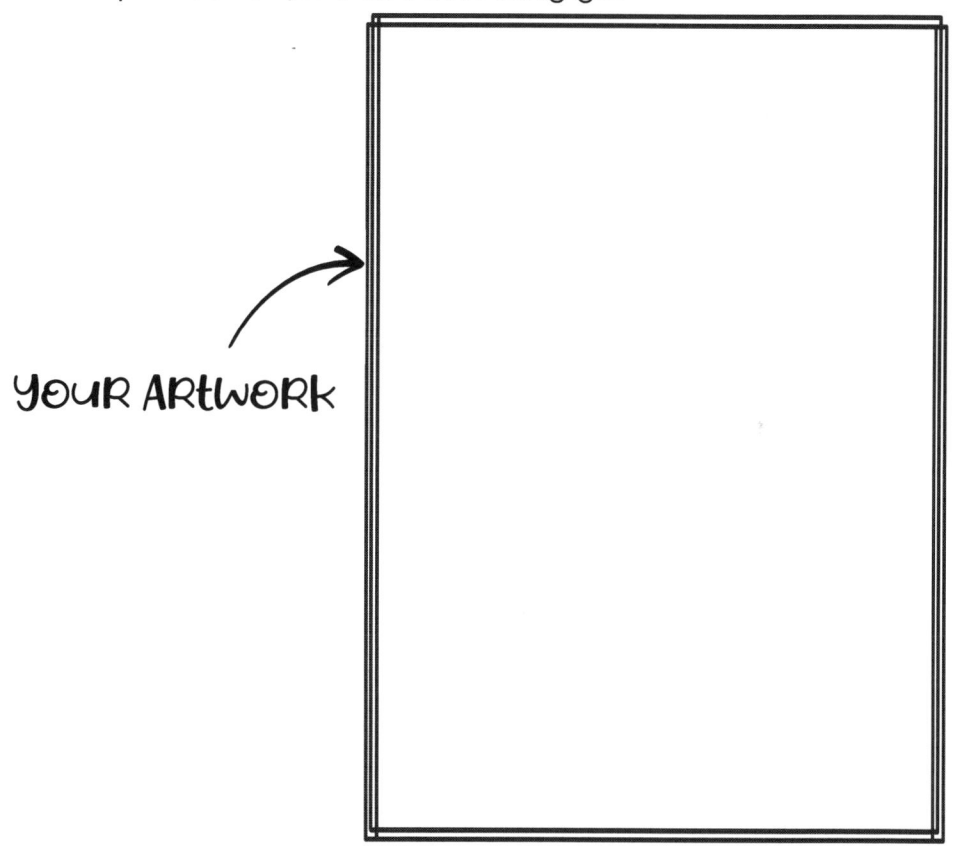

Your Artwork

Make yourself a cup of tea or coffee, play some calming music, and immerse yourself in your own little creative world for a few minutes. This break is for you and your imagination.

56 The Power Smoothie
Energy On-the-Go

Sometimes, you just don't have the energy to tackle the next part of your day. That's where the Power Smoothie comes in – quick, delicious, and packed with ingredients to give you the boost you need.

Recipe for a Quick Power Smoothie:

- 1 banana
- 1 handful of spinach
- 200 ml almond milk (or any milk of your choice)
- 1 tbsp oats
- 1 tsp honey or maple syrup (optional)
- 3-4 ice cubes

Instructions:

1. Combine all ingredients in a blender and mix until smooth.
2. Pour into a glass and enjoy – ideally during a quiet moment just for you.

This smoothie isn't just healthy; it's also your little escape, giving you the strength for whatever comes next.

57 The Mini Wellness Plan
10 Minutes Just for You

You don't need a full spa day to feel pampered. Sometimes, a mini wellness ritual is all it takes to recharge.

Grab your favorite hand cream and slowly massage it into your hands. Focus on the movement, the scent, and the moment that's just for you. Afterward, enjoy a hot cup of tea or coffee and let the world fade away for a moment.

This small gesture is a reminder that even the tiniest acts of self-care can make a big difference – especially when they're just for you.

Completed On:
_____

TO-DO LIST

DATE:

MUST DO

SHOULD DO

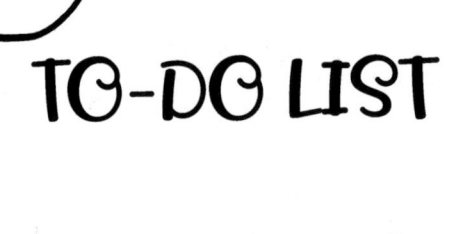

COULD DO

IF I HAVE TIME

TO-DO LIST

DATE:

MUST DO
- [ ] _____
- [ ] _____
- [ ] _____
- [ ] _____
- [ ] _____
- [ ] _____

SHOULD DO
- [ ] _____
- [ ] _____
- [ ] _____
- [ ] _____
- [ ] _____
- [ ] _____

COULD DO
- [ ] _____
- [ ] _____
- [ ] _____
- [ ] _____
- [ ] _____
- [ ] _____

IF I HAVE TIME
- [ ] _____
- [ ] _____
- [ ] _____
- [ ] _____
- [ ] _____
- [ ] _____

58 The Digital Detox
Phone Down, Soul Free

Sometimes, you just need a break from everything – including your phone. Today, try something new: a digital detox.

Put your phone aside for 30 minutes. Turn it on silent, tuck it in a drawer, or place it somewhere out of sight. Use this time for yourself: read a book, enjoy the silence, or simply do nothing.

This moment without constant notifications gives you space to breathe and helps you focus on what truly matters – you. And after the 30 minutes? Check in and see how the world kept spinning without you.

59 The DIY Face Mask
Naturally Beautiful, Mama!

You don't need expensive products – just a few ingredients from your kitchen to treat yourself. A DIY face mask is quick to make and offers a moment of pure relaxation – plus glowing skin.

Recipe for a Honey-Yogurt Mask:

- 2 tbsp plain yogurt
- 1 tsp honey
- 1 tsp lemon juice

Mix the ingredients, apply the mask to your face, and let it sit for 10 minutes. In the meantime, kick back, put your feet up, and enjoy a moment of calm. Then rinse it off and feel the fresh, rejuvenated skin.

This little wellness moment is a reminder of how beautiful and important it is to think about yourself every once in a while.

60 Clear Your Mind, Fill Your Heart
The Evening Walk

After a long, chaotic day, nothing beats clearing your mind with a gentle evening walk. Slip on your comfiest shoes, take a deep breath, and leave the day behind – whether you're walking alone, with your partner, or with the kids.

Evening walks have a certain magic. The world feels calmer, the air cooler, and the movement soothes not only your body but your soul. Use this time to reflect on the day or to simply not think at all – both are equally rewarding.

If the kids are with you, turn it into a game: Who can spot the most stars in the sky? And if you're walking alone, savor the quiet that belongs only to you.

61 The Oven Magic
Baking Bread for the Soul

There's nothing more comforting than the smell of freshly baked bread wafting through the house. Treat yourself to this little magic today – it's easier than you think.

Recipe for Easy No-Knead Bread:

- 500 g flour (e.g., wheat or spelt flour)
- 1 packet of dry yeast
- 1 tsp salt
- 400 ml warm water

Instructions:

1. Mix the flour, yeast, and salt in a bowl.
2. Add the warm water and stir with a spoon until a sticky dough forms.
3. Cover the dough and let it rest for 1–2 hours.
4. Preheat the oven to 200°C (392°F). Place the dough into a greased loaf pan and bake for about 35 minutes.
5. Let it cool and enjoy – whether with butter, jam, or simply on its own.

While the bread bakes, take a moment to put your feet up and enjoy the aroma filling your home, letting it melt away the day's stress.

62 The Mini Meditation
3 Minutes for Inner Peace

When the day challenges you more than usual, a short meditation can help you reconnect with yourself. No experience needed – just a quiet moment for you.

Sit comfortably, close your eyes, and focus on your breath. Inhale deeply through your nose and exhale slowly through your mouth. Count to four as you breathe in, pause briefly, and exhale again. As you breathe, imagine any tension leaving your body with each exhale.

After three minutes, you'll feel your mind clearer, your heart lighter, and the chaos of the day a little less overwhelming.

3 mins

# 63 Pizza Night
Simple, Quick, and Happy

Sometimes, the simplest solution is the best one. A pizza night not only saves your day but also brings smiles to the whole family. And the best part? Homemade always tastes better!

Quick Pizza Dough Recipe:

- 500 g flour
- 1 packet of dry yeast
- 1 tsp salt
- 300 ml warm water
- 2 tbsp olive oil

Instructions:

1. Mix the flour, yeast, and salt in a bowl. Add the water and olive oil, then knead into a smooth dough.
2. Let the dough rest for 30 minutes.
3. Roll it out on parchment paper, top with tomato sauce and your favorite ingredients.
4. Bake at 200°C (392°F) for about 15–20 minutes, until the crust is golden brown.

While the pizza is baking, sit back and enjoy the aroma. And if the family asks why Mom is so relaxed? Just say, "Pizza makes everyone happy – always!"

64 Your Couch, Your Kingdom
A Solo Series Night

There's nothing better than having the evening entirely to yourself. Once the kids are in bed and the house is quiet, the couch is yours – and only yours.

Slip into your comfiest clothes, grab your favorite blanket, and pick a series you've always wanted to watch. Pair it with your snack of choice – chips, popcorn, or even a glass of wine. This evening is all about you, and no interruptions are allowed.

This little luxury reminds you that you're not just a mom but also someone who deserves relaxation and fun. And if the series gets too good? One more episode is always a great idea.

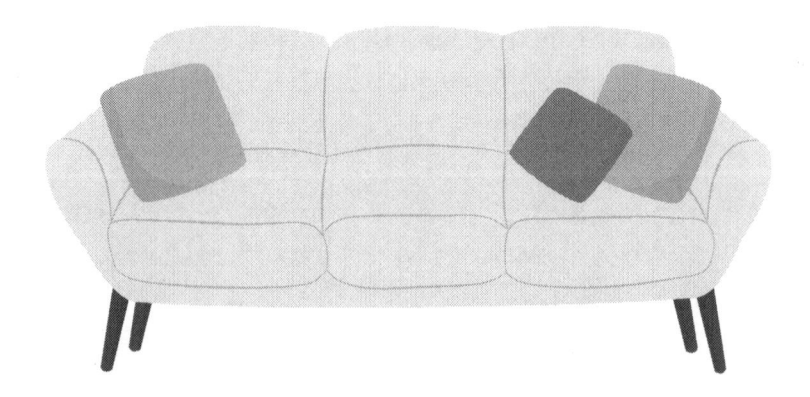

65 The Creativity Magic
Draw and Relax

---- ♥ ---------- ♥ ---------- ♥ ----

A moment of calm, a few pencils, and a blank sheet of paper – sometimes that's all you need to clear your mind and add a little creativity to your day. Today is the perfect time to let your imagination run wild.

Whether you're drawing simple patterns, creating a fun coloring page, or just blending colors together, it's not about the result – it's about the process.

Doodle Space

66 The Morning Coffee Moment
Your Liquid Start to the Day

Sometimes, the first sip of coffee in the morning is more than just a drink – it's the start of a new day and the moment that prepares you for whatever lies ahead.

Make your coffee just the way you like it – maybe black and bold, or with milk and a touch of sugar. Sit in a quiet spot, perhaps by the window, and savor the calm before the chaos of the day begins.

This moment is all yours – before the kids wake up, before the to-do lists start screaming. It's your chance to recharge and remind yourself that you can handle whatever the day throws at you.

All you NEED is Coffee

67 Family Game Night
Laughter, Fun, and Memories

Sometimes, the best way to bring the family together is with a good old-fashioned game night. Put away the screens and break out board games, card games, or fun challenges that everyone will enjoy.

Choose games that everyone loves, from Uno and Sorry! to creative word games like I'm Packing My Suitcase. For older kids, up the difficulty, and for the little ones, simplify the rules to keep it fun.

The goal isn't to win but to laugh together and leave the daily grind behind. And if someone cheats? Even better – it's all part of the fun!

68 Relaxation in Seconds
The Scent of Lavender

Sometimes, a small sensory moment is all you need to shake off the stress of the day. Lavender is your secret helper – calming, soothing, and simple to use.

Fill a small bowl with warm water and add a few drops of lavender oil. Place the bowl nearby while you read, work, or just put your feet up. Alternatively, you can put a few drops on a tissue and inhale the scent whenever you need a quick moment of calm.

The soothing fragrance helps you breathe deeply and regain focus, even when life feels overwhelming. Sometimes, it's the little things that make the biggest difference.

69 The DIY Kids' Cinema
Peace for Mom, Fun for the Kids

There are moments when the kids need an activity that truly captivates them – and gives you a much-needed break. That's exactly what the DIY kids' cinema is for.

Set up their favorite blanket, some pillows, and maybe even a bowl of popcorn. Let them pick a favorite movie (with your approval, of course) and create the feeling of their very own little theater.

While they're engrossed in the film, you can step away, enjoy a cup of tea, or simply put your feet up for a while. It's a win for everyone: the kids are happy, and you get a few well-deserved moments of peace.

70 The Evening Candle
Your Ritual to Close the Day

After a long day, a small moment of reflection can work wonders. Lighting an evening candle is a simple yet powerful ritual to leave the day behind.

Light a candle, find a cozy spot, and take a moment to reflect on the day. What went well? What would you like to do differently tomorrow? The soft glow of the flame helps calm your mind and ease you into a relaxed evening mode.

Perhaps you'll enjoy a cup of tea or jot down a few thoughts in a journal. This little moment gives you the feeling of consciously closing the day – and preparing yourself for a better tomorrow.

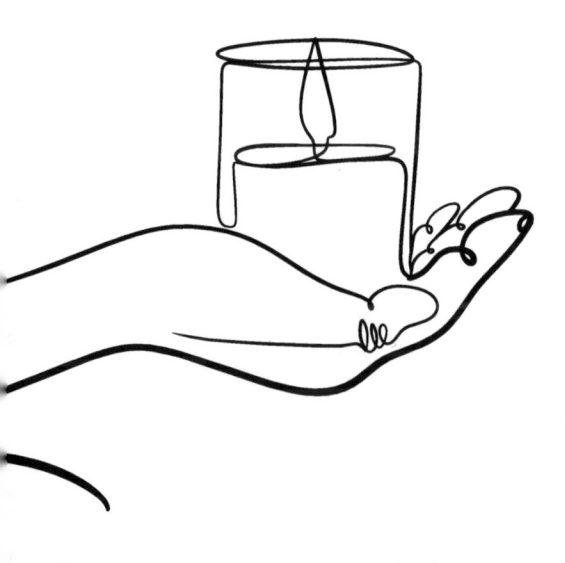

71 The Good-Night Journal
Sorting Thoughts, Finding Calm

A journal can be a wonderful companion for closing the day and sorting through your thoughts. It's your space to write down everything on your mind – free from judgment and pressure.

Grab a beautiful notebook and write a few sentences each night: What went well today? What are you grateful for? What would you like to do differently tomorrow? They don't have to be long entries – sometimes, a simple list or one sentence is enough.

This small moment helps you consciously close the day and go to sleep with a clearer mind. And the best part: your journal becomes a treasure that shows how strong and creative you navigate everyday life.

72 The Snack of Calm
Snack Your Way to Happiness

Sometimes, a small snack is all it takes to give yourself a mini break. Today, it's time for something quick to prepare, delicious, and that sweetens your day for a moment.

Recipe for Quick Apple Snacks with Peanut Butter:

- 1 apple (sliced)
- 2-3 tbsp peanut butter
- A handful of nuts, raisins, or chocolate chips

Spread peanut butter on the apple slices and top with your choice of toppings. Grab your snack, sit down, and enjoy the mix of sweetness and satisfaction. This little moment is all yours – and it tastes as good as it feels.

73 The Gratitude List
Start the Day with Positivity

Amid the chaos of everyday life, there are always a few small things that are going well – and those are the things that belong on your gratitude list. This ritual helps you focus on the positive aspects of life.

Take a few minutes in the morning or evening to write down three things you're grateful for. They can be big or small, like "The sun was shining," "My child made me laugh," or "I had five minutes of peace to myself."

This practice helps you start or end the day with a positive mindset. And if you ever have a bad day? Flip through your old lists and remind yourself that there are always moments of brightness.

Gratitude Journal

S M T W T F S   Date

Today, I am grateful for

1

2

3

JUST BREATHE

Mom's Wishlist
(Example: 1 hour of complete peace)

- [ ] _____
- [ ] _____
- [ ] _____
- [ ] _____
- [ ] _____
- [ ] _____
- [ ] _____
- [ ] _____
- [ ] _____
- [ ] _____
- [ ] _____

I CAN DO THIS

74 The Pampering Tea
A Cup Full of Calm

There's nothing more soothing than holding a hot cup of tea in your hands. It warms not only your body but also your soul – perfect for a little break in the hectic pace of everyday life.

Pick your favorite tea, whether it's calming chamomile, refreshing mint, or a spicy chai. Pour it into your cup, sit in your favorite spot, and breathe in the aroma deeply. This moment is all yours – no interruptions, no to-do lists, just you and your tea.

Let the world wait outside for a few minutes. Because this little break is a gift you give yourself.

75 The Music of Relaxation
Your Personal Playlist

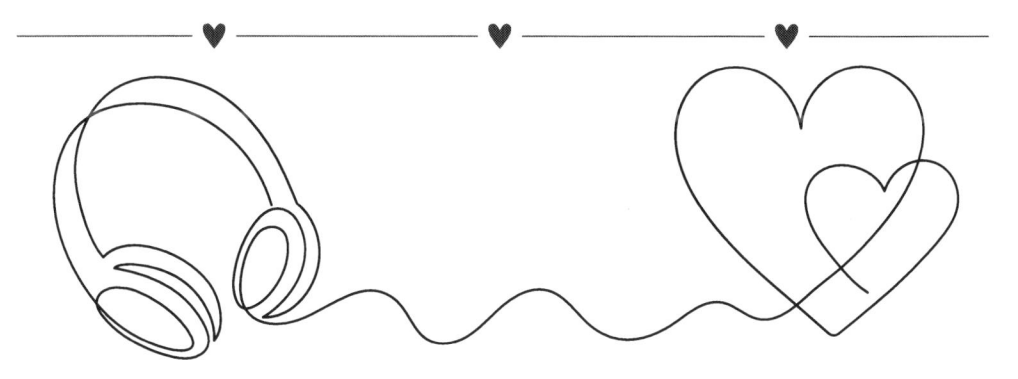

Music has the power to make everything better – including your everyday life. Create a playlist with your absolute favorite songs that relax, motivate, or simply make you happy.

Turn it on while you're cooking, cleaning, or just putting your feet up. Let the melodies carry you, sing along, or dance if the mood strikes. The playlist is your soundtrack for the moment when you allow yourself to simply enjoy.

And if the kids ask for their music? Tell them it's Mama DJ time – because every now and then, you get to set the tone.

76 The Fresh Air Moment
Window Open, Mind Clear

Sometimes, all it takes is opening the window to enjoy the fresh air and find a moment of peace. Stand by the window, take a deep breath, and let the sounds of the outside world wash over you – birds chirping, the wind blowing, or the distant hum of the city.

If you'd like, grab a cup of tea or coffee and savor the break. Look outside and let your thoughts drift for a moment, just like the clouds in the sky.

This small fresh air moment works wonders, whether you live on the 3rd floor or the ground floor. It's your breath of freedom in the middle of the everyday hustle.

77 The Everyday Song
Singing Makes You Happy

It's scientifically proven: Singing boosts your mood, reduces stress, and gives you an energy boost – whether you're a pro or just a shower singer. Today is the perfect day to try out your voice.

Pick a favorite song, turn up the volume (or sing quietly just for yourself), and let the notes flow. It's not about perfection; it's about having fun. You can sing in the shower, while cooking, or simply in the living room.

And if the kids want to join in? Even better! Turn it into a little family concert and celebrate the joyful sounds – even if they're off-key.

78 The Feel-Good Card
Write Yourself Happy

Sometimes, making someone else happy is all it takes to feel a little happier yourself. Write a small card or letter to someone dear to you – a friend, your parents, or even your kids.

It doesn't have to be anything big. A few kind words like "Thank you for always being there for me" or "I just wanted to tell you how much I appreciate you" are more than enough. These small gestures will not only put a smile on the recipient's face but also on yours.

And who says you can't write a card to yourself? A few motivating words or a reminder of how amazing you are might just be exactly what you need.

79 The Mini Kitchen
Cooking with Kids Made Easy

Sometimes, the little ones need an activity that excites them – and the kitchen is the perfect place for it. Today, you'll cook a simple dish together that's not only delicious but also fun.

Recipe: Homemade Fruit Skewers

- Various fruits (e.g., apples, bananas, grapes, melon)
- Wooden skewers
- Optional: chocolate sauce or yogurt for dipping

Let the kids cut the fruit into small pieces (depending on their age, using a child-safe knife) and thread them onto the skewers. The result is a colorful snack that's not only healthy but also a fun treat.

While the kids get creative, you can enjoy a small break – or join in and enjoy the fun together.

80 Letting Go of Thoughts
The Creative Writing Moment

Sometimes, it helps to just get your thoughts down on paper – freely, without rules, just for you. Grab a notebook (or use this space) and write down whatever comes to mind: funny experiences, reflections on your day, or simply words that pop into your head.

If you like, turn it into short stories or poems. It's not about perfection, but about sorting your mind and letting your thoughts flow. In the end, you'll not only have a clearer head but maybe something beautiful that'll make you smile later.

....
....
....
....
....
....
....
....
....
....
....

81 Your Movie, Your Rules
The Home Cinema for Mom

After a long day, there's nothing better than curling up on the couch and choosing a movie just for yourself. No kids' movies, no debates – today, you pick the program.

Make a bowl of popcorn or grab a piece of your favorite chocolate, slip into your coziest clothes, and let the movie night begin. Whether you choose a romantic comedy, a thrilling suspense film, or an inspiring documentary – this evening is all about you.

Sometimes, just diving into another world for two hours is all you need to recharge for the next day.

Watched Movie

82 A Sweet Break
The Smell of Freshly Baked Cookies

Baking is not only a way to create something delicious, but also a wonderful opportunity to clear your mind. Today, it's time for quick and easy cookies that fill your kitchen with their scent and bring a smile to everyone's face.

Recipe for Simple Vanilla Cookies:

- 200 g flour
- 100 g sugar
- 100 g butter (soft)
- 1 egg
- 1 tsp vanilla sugar

Instructions:

1. Mix all ingredients in a bowl to form a smooth dough.
2. Shape the dough into small balls, place them on a baking sheet, and flatten them slightly.
3. Bake at 180°C (356°F, top/bottom heat) for about 10-12 minutes, until the cookies are golden.
4. Let them cool and enjoy – ideally with a cup of tea or coffee.

While the cookies are baking, put your feet up and enjoy the delightful scent filling your home.

83 Creating Memories
The Picture Frame Moment

In the hustle and bustle of everyday life, we often forget how many wonderful moments we've already experienced. Today is the perfect opportunity to remember and capture these special moments.

Pick out a few photos that are especially close to your heart – from family outings, funny moments, or simple everyday scenes. Print them out or find a picture frame that's been empty for too long, and give these memories a place in your home.

The best part: As you look through and choose the photos, you'll feel how the beautiful moments fill you with energy and gratitude. And the finished pictures on the wall? They'll remind you every day of all the goodness that's already there.

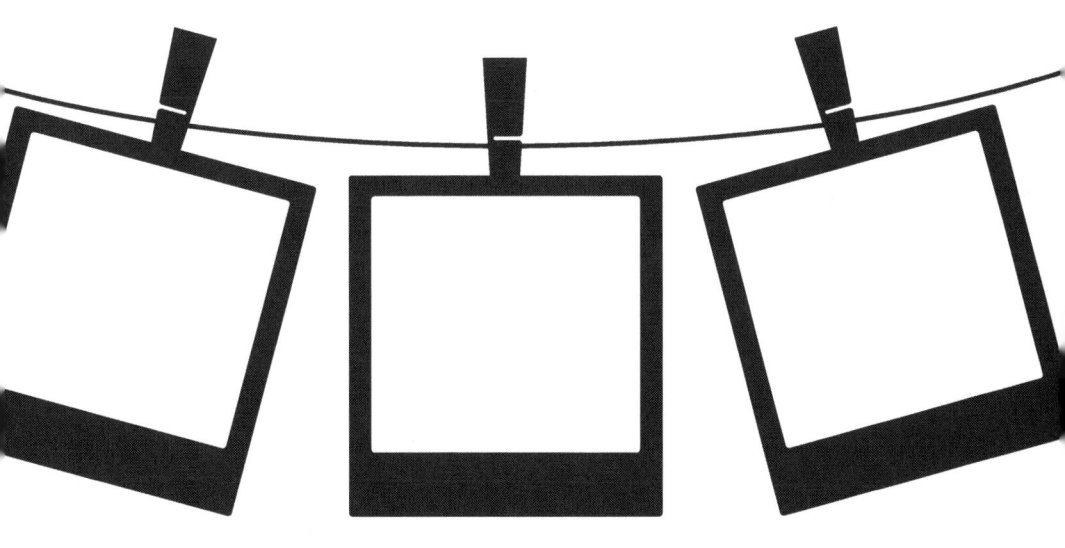

84 The Aromatherapy Break
Relaxation Through Scents

A soothing scent can work wonders when life gets too hectic. With just a few drops of essential oil, you can quickly create your own little oasis of calm.

Choose an essential oil that appeals to you – lavender for relaxation, lemon for freshness, or vanilla for coziness. Add a few drops to an oil diffuser, a tissue, or a bowl of warm water. Close your eyes and breathe in the scent deeply.

This small moment helps you center yourself, breathe deeply, and regain balance – all without much effort.

85 Relaxation with Letters
Word Search for a Quick Break

Sometimes, the perfect way to clear your mind is with a small puzzle. This word search brings fun and relaxation - ideal for a little mom break.

```
U T Q B V Y D Z T I N O G N N D C I U J
S M N J R I R I V P E I Y O E A O O L K
H B J W U R M A H Q B B K S R I J C Z D
F A J Q O E B W M M L B B A J B H L W M
T C V G O Z M A C F I A K C O S O O C X
S E Q U U K P N B Z I N C A V V D T W B
V C T E E A G F V U K W E L O M E H K R
A Y J E C N L H P J K S O L H P O E Q F
H T F G L Q B S Q V Z I R L O A U S L M
B C Q R J M A W D W N T L P L T R H W S
T M Y L S A Z U P I P B I G I I E P Y O
S R C E A E B C H A K I G Z Q E P L L B
L E A S F Y L J H E G E H J G N M V Y F
J L O S S K F F L N A C T T S C E I H W
G E E P M C A H C G K A A R Z E B Z T P
P G D X N A L P C A M D V L Z D M B N G
M P X W E Y J O W Y R I C R M V J O U D
F Z R D X T K N M K E E G L E Q E I Z H
A S J C G X I Z Q H U U O E H V X Z E F
Q B H D W Z X D T T F P N A E I S Q E A
```

CALM
LIGHT
SELF-CARE

CLOTHES
PATIENCE
TIME

KIDS
PILLOW
TIME-OUT

Plan Your Day

Today's Schedule:

05:00

06:00

07:00

08:00

09:00

10:00

11:00

12:00

13:00

14:00

15:00

16:00

17:00

18:00

19:00

20:00

21:00

22:00

23:00

Plan Your Day

(Top Priorities of the Day)

- ○ _____
- ○ _____
- ○ _____
- ○ _____
- ○ _____

Water Intake

◊◊◊◊ / ◊◊◊◊ / ◊◊◊◊
  1L   2L   3L

(Calls/Emails)

- ○ _____
- ○ _____
- ○ _____
- ○ _____
- ○ _____

What made you happy today?

86 The Feel-Good Coloring Page
Creativity for the Soul

Sometimes, all you need is a few colors and a quiet spot to clear your mind. A coloring page is perfect for letting your creativity flow and forgetting the stress of the day.

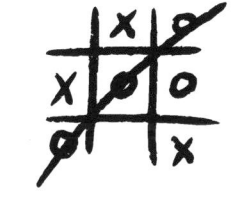

87 The Classic Game
Tic-Tac-Toe for a Quick Break

Sometimes, all it takes is a simple game to unwind for a few minutes or keep the kids entertained. Tic-Tac-Toe is perfect: quick, easy, and guaranteed fun.

Draw the classic grid (three by three squares) on a piece of paper, and you're ready to go. Whether playing against the kids, your partner, or just taking a creative break for yourself, this little game brings smiles with no effort required.

Make it more exciting by adding special rules: The winner gets to choose what's for dinner, or the loser has to clean up the toys.

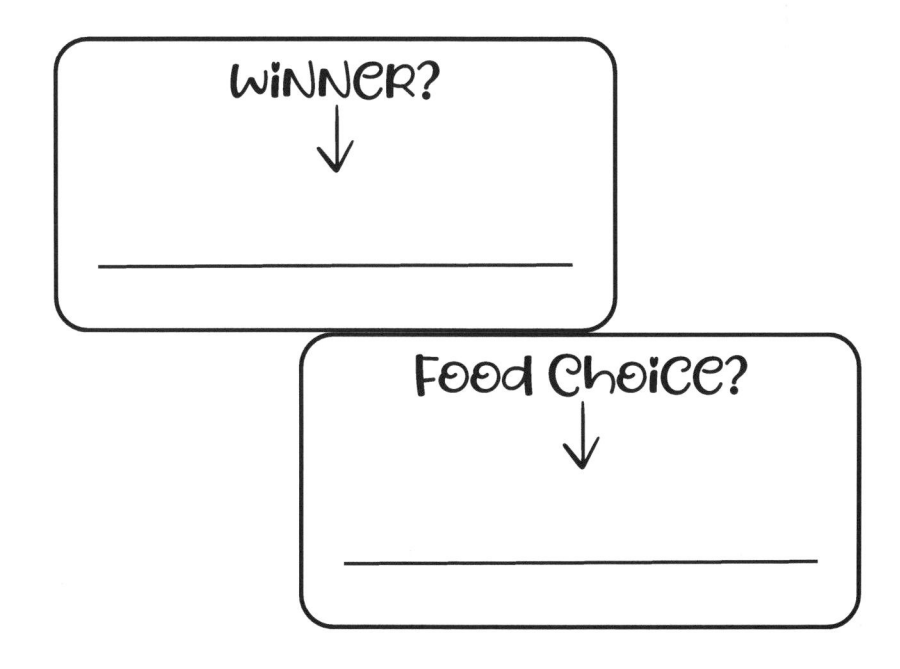

Winner?
↓
_____

Food Choice?
↓
_____

88 Sudoku Magic
Number Logic for Your Break

Sometimes, a Sudoku puzzle is just what you need to clear your mind. This little number game relaxes, challenges, and gives you a moment to focus solely on yourself.
Sit down with a pen and a cup of tea in your favorite spot, and let the numbers speak to you.

			3			9		5
9				7			3	
3			9	5	1			8
6				9	4		5	
1	9						7	3
	8		7	1				2
8			5	2	6			7
	7			8				6
2		1			7			

89 The Quick Kitchen
A Fast Snack for New Energy

Sometimes, a small snack is all it takes to regain control of the day. Today, we're making quick cucumber bites – fresh, tasty, and super easy.

Recipe for Cucumber Bites:

- 1 cucumber
- Cream cheese (plain or herb)
- Optional: smoked salmon, ham, or tomato slices

Instructions:

1. Slice the cucumber into thick rounds.
2. Spread cream cheese on each slice.
3. Top with smoked salmon, ham, or tomatoes as desired.

This little snack is not only healthy but also perfect for taking a quick break and recharging. And if the kids want to help? Let them get creative with the toppings – it's fun and tastes even better.

90 The DIY Herbal Tea
A Feel-Good Moment from the Kitchen

Homemade herbal tea is not only delicious, but also a small wellness moment that you can easily create at home.

Recipe for DIY Herbal Tea:

- 1 tsp dried chamomile flowers
- 1 tsp mint leaves (dried or fresh)
- 1 piece of ginger (finely chopped)
- 250 ml hot water
- Optional: a spoonful of honey

Place the herbs and ginger in a teapot, pour hot water over them, and let the tea steep for 5 minutes. Pour it into your favorite cup, sit in a quiet spot, and enjoy the scent and warmth.

This little moment is all yours – a sip of relaxation, directly from nature.

91 The Creative Puzzle Fun
your Personal Crossword

A crossword puzzle is the perfect mix of relaxation and mental exercise – and just what you need to tune out the everyday hustle for a few minutes.

```
G N V Y Y K I P M J M N S K X A D E P H
T Y Z G L S U D U H Z Q Z C W U A O F R
T U K H P B A D S Z M E R U S I E L C A
H S W M W D H Q Y X Z H E L R G O O E A
X E C M G O D O J Y A L S Q K S N P L S
V Q A W J H X C F Z C W E P B T K A J B
W G R D D H C X F S Y C D S E S D W O W
U K P E C O N J A E Y P R N H V P T Z S
T E A T A U U R I D Y O T E E C N V O Y
L Z T M Y S Z X L N W M F N A G U U R Q
A C Z O C E K K X Z E T T L I T R W Y W
W Z D T M H R L B N P U Z W Y U I H R T
M A B I C O A Q T C R E I P K T H V Q V
R V A V U L J F H O K U Y D K P N I E Z
T Z S A F D S D U I T T D V K C Y Q D A
J T S T T L V S W I O E L U K U P Z V J
K O B I J E W T E X J F G E Y C B Z O T
Q D X O D Y S X L V Z V Y P T X D R Y V
U X F N H R X D Z H L Y L F U N N Y I G
M A I X B I Y Z M M O U Q A A X T J B Y
```

ADVENTUROUS	CONTENTMENT	CREATIVE
FUNNY	HOUSEHOLD	LEISURE
MOTIVATION	PUZZLES	TEA

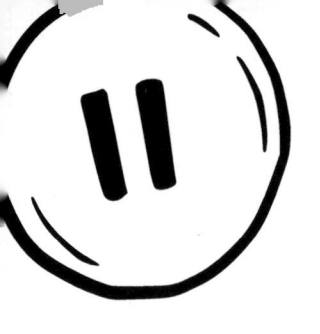

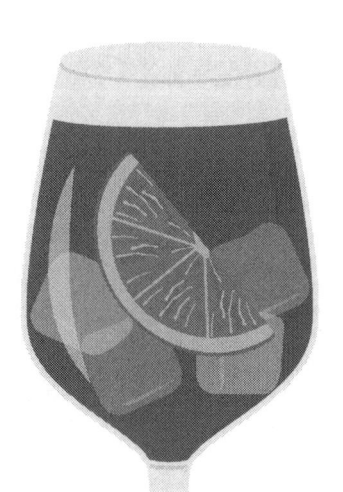

Aperol Spritz

Ingredients:
3 parts Prosecco
2 parts Aperol
1 part soda water
Ice cubes
Orange slice (for garnish)

Instructions:
Fill a glass with ice cubes.
Add Prosecco, Aperol, and soda water.
Stir gently and garnish with an orange slice.

gin & tonic

Ingredients:
50 ml gin
150 ml tonic water
Ice cubes
Lime slice or zest (for garnish)

Instructions:
Fill a glass with ice cubes. Pour in the gin and top with tonic water. Stir gently and garnish with a lime slice.

92 Wellness for Your Hands
The DIY Hand Scrub Moment

Between cooking, cleaning, and countless to-dos, your hands deserve a little break too. A homemade hand scrub is the perfect way to pamper them and treat yourself to a small wellness moment.

Recipe for a Quick Hand Scrub:

- 2 tbsp sugar
- 1 tbsp olive oil
- A few drops of lemon juice

Mix the ingredients in a small bowl. Gently rub the scrub into your hands, massage it in briefly, and then rinse off with warm water. Your hands will feel soft and nourished – and you've more than earned this little break.

93 The Family Story Game
Getting Creative Together

Sometimes, all it takes is a little imagination to excite the family and forget about the everyday routine. The Story Game is perfect for this, turning everyone into storytellers.

How It Works:

One person starts with a sentence, e.g., "Once upon a time, there was a talking shoe that lived in a rainbow." The next person adds a sentence that continues the story. Everyone takes turns adding to the tale until a funny, crazy, or even exciting story unfolds.

The game will have everyone laughing and is a wonderful way to be creative together. In the end, you can even write the story down – who knows, you might have just invented the next children's book!

94 The Mini Library
Reading Time for Mom

Amidst the chaos of everyday life, a good book is like a little escape into another world. Today, it's time to explore your mini-library – even if it's just one book on your nightstand.

Find a quiet spot, grab your current favorite book, and dive in. Whether for just five minutes or a whole hour, it doesn't matter. What matters is that this moment is all yours.

And if the kids ask why you're so absorbed? Tell them that Mom is a heroine in a story right now – and heroes need some peace to conquer their adventures.

Book Read?
↓
_____

95 Baking for the Soul
The Feel-Good Cake

There are days when a cake is the perfect solution – not just for eating, but as a calming ritual. Baking relaxes you, gives you structure, and in the end, you have something sweet that brightens your day.

Recipe for a Quick Chocolate Cake:

- 200 g flour
- 150 g sugar
- 50 g cocoa powder
- 100 ml oil
- 200 ml milk
- 1 packet baking powder

Instructions:

1. Combine all ingredients in a bowl and mix into a smooth batter.
2. Pour the batter into a greased baking pan and bake at 180°C (356°F, top/bottom heat) for about 25 minutes.
3. Let it cool and enjoy – ideally with a cup of coffee or tea.

While the cake is baking, put your feet up and look forward to the scent filling the kitchen. A sweet moment that gives you energy for the rest of the day.

96 The Starry Sky Moment
Peace Under the Open Sky

Sometimes, the best way to escape the everyday is by looking up at the night sky. Throw a blanket over your shoulders, grab a warm drink, and step outside or sit by the window. The starry sky reminds you of how vast the world is and how small your problems can seem in comparison.

If you like, you can look for constellations or simply enjoy the silence. And if the kids are with you, turn it into a little game: Who spots the Big Dipper first?

This moment under the vast sky gives you not only peace but also a special connection to nature – and to yourself.

97 The Crafting Break
Creativity with Paper and Scissors

Sometimes, crafting is the perfect way to clear your mind and create something beautiful – whether alone or with the kids. Today, we're making a simple paper heart for window decoration.

You'll need:

- Colored paper
- Scissors
- Glue or tape
- Optional: Markers or glitter for decoration

Instructions:

1. Cut out a large heart from the colored paper.
2. Decorate it with drawings, patterns, or glitter as you like.
3. Hang it on the window or any spot that brings you joy.

Crafting helps sort your thoughts, and the finished heart will bring a smile every time you see it. And if the kids join in, you might end up with a whole window full of love.

98 Breakfast in Bed
The Relaxed Morning

Want to feel like you're in a hotel? You can do that at home – with breakfast in bed. Whether alone, with your partner, or even with the kids, this special start to the day brings relaxation and good vibes.

Prepare a tray with everything you love: fresh rolls, jam, fruit, a boiled egg, and of course, a cup of coffee or tea. Sit comfortably in bed, surrounded by pillows, and enjoy the moment.

If the kids are with you, turn it into a little picnic. And if you're alone, relish the quiet and the feeling of pampering yourself.

99 The Lucky Stone Moment
A Small Ritual for Positive Energy

A lucky stone is more than just a pretty piece of nature – it can be a companion that reminds you of positive thoughts and gives you strength.

Find a special stone, whether from your garden, your last vacation, or even from a craft store. Hold it in your hand when you're feeling stressed, and let your worries "flow" into it. You can also paint it with a positive message, like "Calm" or "Strength."

Place the stone somewhere you'll see it often – on your nightstand, by the window, or in your bag. This small moment of connection with a simple object helps you regain focus in stressful moments.

100 Deluxe Foot Bath
The Mini Wellness Moment

Sometimes, a foot bath is all it takes to feel rejuvenated. It's simple, quick to prepare, and gives you a moment of pure relaxation – just what you need after a long day.

What you need:

- A bowl of warm water
- 2 tbsp coarse salt
- A few drops of essential oil (e.g., lavender or mint)
- Optional: A towel to keep warm
-

Add the ingredients to the water, sit in a cozy spot, and dip your feet in. Close your eyes, take a deep breath, and let the warmth draw out the tension from your body.

After 10 minutes, you'll feel refreshed, relaxed, and ready to enjoy the rest of your day – or simply go to bed.

101 The Power Nap
Energy in 20 Minutes

Sometimes, the best thing you can do is simply close your eyes for a moment and leave the hustle and bustle of daily life behind. A 20-minute power nap is enough to recharge your energy and tackle the rest of the day with renewed vigor.

Grab a blanket, lie down on the couch or in bed, and set a timer for exactly 20 minutes. Too long? No worries – even 10 minutes can work wonders. The key is not to overdo it: it's all about taking a short moment to let go and relax.

And if the kids ask why mom is sleeping? Tell them that superpowers need to be recharged – they'll understand.

102 Photo Album, But Different
The Memory Lookback

In between the many tasks of everyday life, it's worth taking a moment to pause and reflect on the beautiful moments. Today, you'll create a little retrospective – whether digital or with physical photos.

Grab an old photo album or open the photo gallery on your phone and select a few special pictures. Maybe you'll organize them in an album, print them out, or make a small collage. While doing this, you'll be reminded of how many wonderful moments you've had – and that makes even the stressful days a little lighter.

If the kids want to join in, make it a shared project: Each family member picks their favorite photos and explains why these moments are special.

103 The 5-Minute Break — Just Do Nothing

Sometimes, the simplest way to relax is by doing absolutely nothing. No tasks, no appointments – just you and a few minutes of total quiet.

Find a comfortable spot, sit down, close your eyes, and take a deep breath in and out. Let the daily hustle wait outside for five minutes, and simply enjoy the silence. No thoughts about laundry, dinner, or the next task – this moment is all yours.

This mini moment helps you recharge and clear your mind before diving back into the everyday routine.

Completed on:
↓
_____

104 The Mini Massage Moment
Neck Relaxation

After a long day, the neck is often the area that feels the most tense. A small self-massage can work wonders and help you loosen up and relax.

Take 5 minutes, sit up straight, and gently massage your neck with both hands. Use small circular movements, slowly working your way up the neck to the shoulders.

Make sure to keep the movements calm and even. For an even deeper massage, you can wrap a tennis ball in a towel and gently roll it over your neck.

This small moment of self-care gives you the feeling of turning away from the stress of the day and recharging your energy.

relax

105 The Mini Art Break
Drawing for the Moment

When your mind is overflowing and the daily grind is overwhelming, sometimes the best thing you can do is simply grab a pen and put something on paper – without a goal, without pressure. Today is the moment to just start drawing whatever comes to mind.

Whether it's simple lines, a doodle, or a funny face – it's not about the outcome, but about the process. Sit comfortably, grab a pen, and let your creativity flow. You'll notice how this small moment of relaxation helps clear your mind.

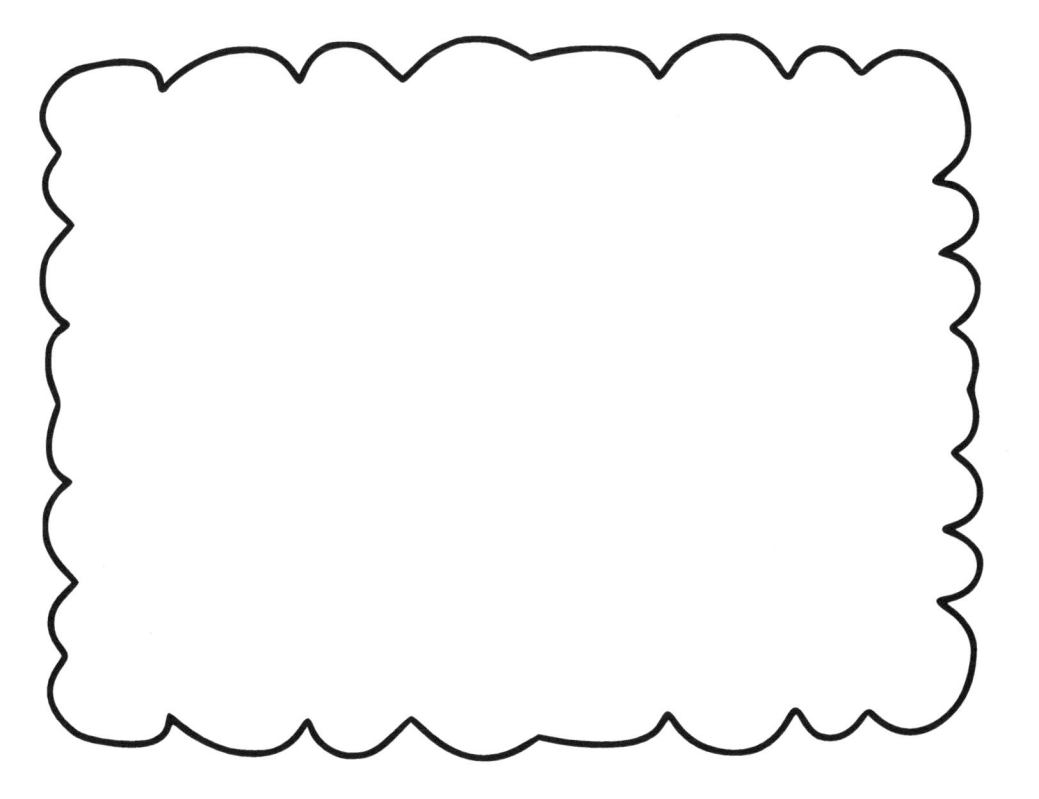

I AM ENOUGH!

Here are some affirmations divided into various themes such as money, success, and health:

Self-Confidence

1. "I trust myself and my abilities."
2. "I am strong, courageous, and capable of overcoming any obstacle."
3. "I believe in myself and my decisions."
4. "I am proud of the person I am today."
5. "I am confident and move forward with certainty."
6. "I have everything I need to be successful."
7. "I allow myself to shine and be successful."
8. "I have faith in my path and my future."

Love and Relationships

1. "I deserve to be loved and respected."
2. "I attract loving and healthy relationships."
3. "I am open to deep and fulfilling connections."
4. "My relationships are based on trust, love, and understanding."
5. "I communicate with love and openness."
6. "I value and respect myself, and this is reflected in my relationships."
7. "I allow love in without fear or doubt."
8. "I am grateful for the love that surrounds me."

I AM ENOUGH!

Success in Career and Work

1. "I am successful in everything I do."
2. "I attract career opportunities that help me grow."
3. "I work with passion and dedication, which brings me success."
4. "I am ready to take on new career challenges."
5. "I seize opportunities and move forward boldly."
6. "I deserve professional success and recognition."
7. "Every step I take brings me closer to my goal."
8. "I am a magnet for career opportunities and positive outcomes."

Health and Well-being

1. "I take good care of my body and health."
2. "Every day brings me more energy and vitality."
3. "I enjoy feeling healthy and strong."
4. "I listen to my body and give it what it needs."
5. "My health is my top priority."
6. "I make healthy choices every day that strengthen me."
7. "I am grateful for my body and everything it does for me."
8. "My body is full of energy and in perfect balance."

106 The Mini Movie Moment
A Short Break for you

Sometimes, all it takes is 10 minutes to recharge – and what could be better than a short movie clip or a funny scene from your favorite series? You don't need to watch an entire film, just a scene that makes you laugh or gives you a brief moment of joy.

Pick your favorite clip, turn on the TV or your phone, and dive briefly into the story. These small breaks can work wonders, helping you continue with fresh energy. And if the kids ask what you're watching? "Just something that makes me happy!"

107 Scents for the Soul
The Aromatherapy Moment

Scents have an incredible power to influence our well-being. Sometimes, all it takes is a pleasant fragrance to clear your mind and banish the stress of the day.

Treat yourself to a little aromatherapy moment: light a scented candle or use essential oils. You can also use a diffuser or add a few drops to a handkerchief. Choose calming scents like lavender, chamomile, or citrus fruits.

The scent will surround you as you sit back, breathe deeply, and let everything else fade away for a moment. You'll be amazed at how quickly your mood calms, and the everyday hustle moves to the background.

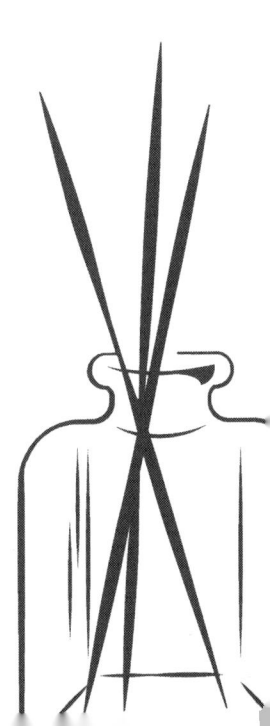

108 The Nature Moment
A Glimpse of Green

It doesn't always have to be a long walk in the park – sometimes, all it takes is simply looking outside and observing nature.

Sit by the window or step onto the balcony, and let your gaze wander over the greenery. Look at the trees, watch the birds, or just listen to the wind rustling. This small moment of stillness allows you to momentarily forget the hectic pace of everyday life and gives you new energy.

And if you don't have plants nearby, a look at the sky can work wonders – the clouds, the sunset, or the gentle morning light can be just as calming.

109 The Power 10 Minutes
Quick and Effective Relaxation

It doesn't always have to be a long moment of relaxation – sometimes, just 10 minutes are enough to recharge and clear your mind.

Turn off all distractions and find a quiet spot.

Set a timer for 10 minutes and focus on something simple that brings you joy: perhaps reading a few pages of a book, enjoying a cup of coffee, or just breathing deeply and soaking in the silence.

10 minutes can be incredibly refreshing – the perfect small break to chase away stress and continue with fresh energy.

GOOD VIBES

110 The Creative Moment
A Doodle for the Soul

When your mind is full and the stress is getting louder, it often helps to just grab a pen and draw – without a plan, without pressure, simply from the gut.

Grab a piece of paper and some colored pencils or a pen, and start doodling. Whether it's simple lines, patterns, or funny figures – the goal is not to create art, but to let go.

Maybe funny pictures will emerge that make you smile, or you'll create something unexpected that brightens the moment.

This small break not only sparks creativity but also gives you the feeling of being in the present, without thinking about the to-do list.

111 The "I Did It" Moment

At the end of the book, the most important moment awaits you: **the moment of pride**. You've made it through 111 ways to survive the madness of motherhood, you've laughed, relaxed, and sometimes just done nothing at all. And that's a reason to celebrate.

Take a moment to reflect on everything you've accomplished – as a mom, as a woman, as a person. You've found your own way to survive the chaos of everyday life, and that's a huge achievement. Be proud of yourself.

Imagine holding your own award in your hand – for all the moments when you took care of yourself. And when the day is particularly tough again, remember this moment when you cared for yourself.

You did it – and that's an accomplishment that deserves to be celebrated.

✓ DONE

Final Words:
A Reminder to Yourself

Congratulations! You did it – 111 ways to survive the madness of motherhood, and you've accompanied yourself on this adventure. You've laughed, found time to relax, discovered creative breaks, and continually reminded yourself that you deserve a pause, too.

Balancing the many tasks of life isn't easy, especially as a mom. Yet here you are, full of energy, with countless ideas and a wonderful toolkit of ways to navigate through the daily challenges. And that's the point: You're not alone in the madness of motherhood. There will be countless moments in life that will challenge you – but there are just as many moments that will strengthen you and show you how valuable you are.

So remember: It's okay to say "no" sometimes and take a break. No one expects you to be perfect. You are already amazing, just as you are. You are the heroine of your everyday life, and you should be proud of what you do – day in and day out.

The little and big moments you fill with your smile are ones you'll never want to miss. And when the madness of motherhood strikes again, simply return to these ways and remember all the powerful, fun, creative, and calming things that helped you face your everyday life with a smile.

Motivational Farewell: You Are a Hero

The path you're walking now isn't always easy. But you've shown that with humor, strength, and a big dose of self-care, you can handle anything that comes your way. You are a hero, every single day, and you should be proud of everything you accomplish – both the big and the small.

There are days when the madness of motherhood is especially loud, when the challenges seem endless, and when it feels like you'll never have enough time for yourself.

But that's okay. You're not alone. You've learned to appreciate yourself and take breaks – and that's the true key to success. Because you can only be there for others when you take care of yourself.

The journey continues – and not only will you survive it, but you will keep rocking it. Because you are the best mom for your kids, and you're the best version of yourself when you take the time for the rest you deserve. So keep taking life into your hands, look at your "111 Ways," and remember that you are strong, beautiful, and incredibly valuable. You are the hero of your own life – and that deserves applause.

Encouragement for the Future: You've Got This

This book was just the beginning, the first step towards taking better care of yourself. You now have a collection of ways to survive the madness of motherhood. But the true magic lies in putting them into practice – in the repetition and constant reminder of how important it is to look after yourself.

The tips and methods are here, but true success comes from integrating them into your daily life. Whether you take just 5 minutes or an hour for yourself, every time you focus on self-care, you're making a huge step in the right direction. Be patient with yourself, celebrate the small victories, and remember that you can always return to these ways when the madness of motherhood catches up with you.

Use the knowledge from this book to make your life brighter, happier, and more relaxed. It's never too late to give yourself the space you need. You are the most important person in your life – and you have everything you need to navigate through the everyday chaos. Believe in yourself and your ability to master it all. You've got this – again and again!

I am brave

Thank you: you are incredible!

---♥---------♥---------♥---

Thank you for taking the time to pamper yourself, laugh, and discover new ways to survive the madness of motherhood. You've navigated through 111 ways, finding fresh perspectives and small moments of relaxation along the way. For that, you are already a winner.

This moment is for you. You've encouraged yourself to make the most of each day – and even when you need a break, remember this: You deserve these moments of peace and happiness. It's perfectly okay not to do everything perfectly. What matters is that you stay true to yourself and continue to stand up for you.

You are not just a mom – you are an incredible woman who accomplishes something special every day. Stay true to yourself, keep caring for yourself, and always remember how much you do for both your family and yourself. You are wonderful.

Looking Ahead: Your Journey Continues

Now that you've finished the book, take a moment to reflect: Which path helped you the most? Which exercise do you want to incorporate into your daily routine? What small rituals can you implement each day to do something good for yourself?

Remember, everything you've learned here is something you can carry into your everyday life. These ways are not just thoughts in a book—they are a toolbox that you can open whenever you need it. You are the expert of your own life, and this book has only given you the encouragement to appreciate yourself even more.

Celebrate the small successes that you implement into your daily life, and always make time for yourself—the mom who is the heart of the family and who also keeps a heart full of love for herself.

Build your own Future

Best Mom in the world

Oh, Right ... The Solutions

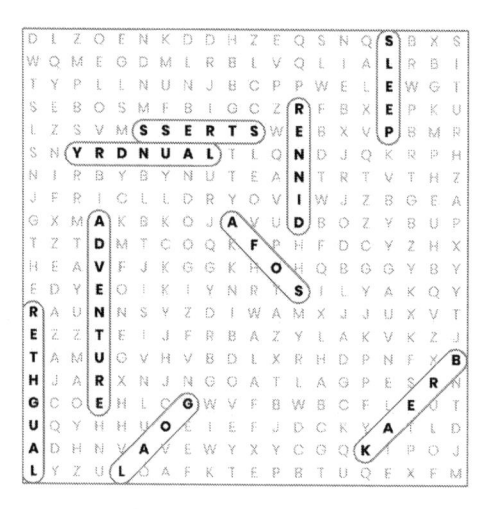

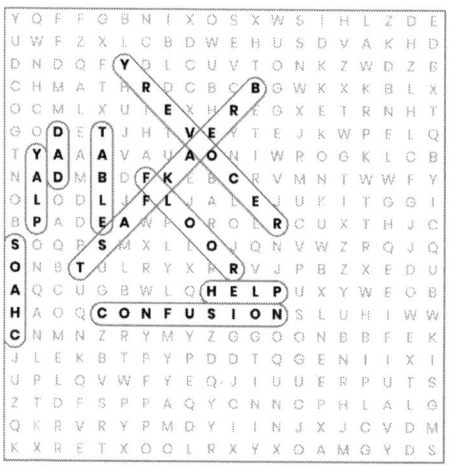

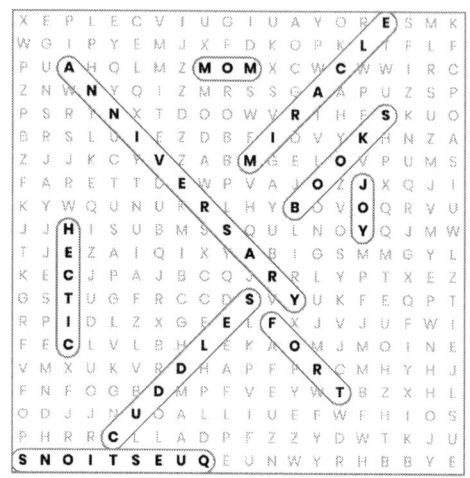

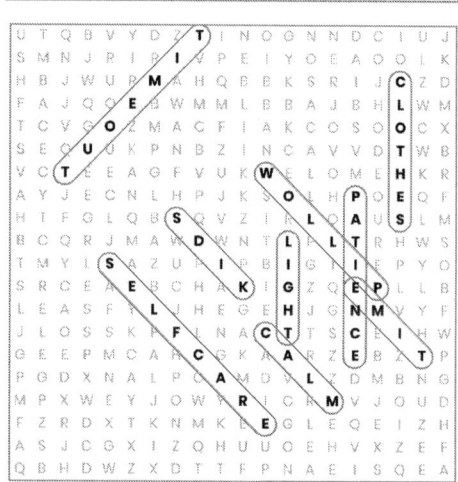

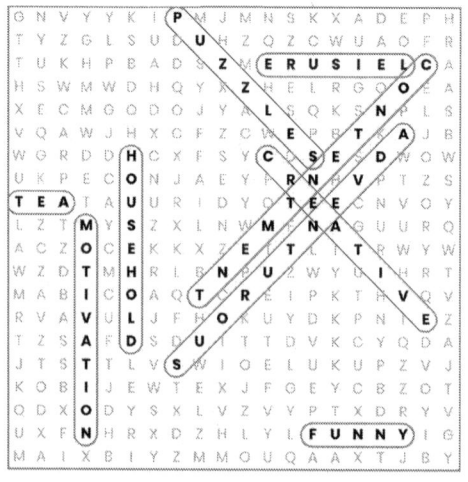

7	3	9	6	5	8	1	2	4
6	4	5	9	1	2	8	7	3
1	8	2	3	7	4	9	6	5
8	7	3	2	4	1	6	5	9
2	6	1	5	9	7	4	3	8
9	5	4	8	3	6	2	1	7
5	1	8	7	6	9	3	4	2
4	9	7	1	2	3	5	8	6
3	2	6	4	8	5	7	9	1

6	1	7	9	4	5	2	3	8
8	3	9	2	6	7	1	4	5
2	5	4	1	8	3	7	6	9
5	4	2	7	3	1	8	9	6
1	9	8	4	5	6	3	2	7
3	7	6	8	9	2	4	5	1
9	2	1	6	7	4	5	8	3
7	6	3	5	2	8	9	1	4
4	8	5	3	1	9	6	7	2

8	7	5	2	4	1	9	6	3
6	2	4	3	9	8	7	1	5
3	1	9	7	6	5	8	2	4
4	5	6	9	7	2	1	3	8
2	8	1	5	3	6	4	7	9
7	9	3	8	1	4	2	5	6
1	6	2	4	5	9	3	8	7
5	4	7	1	8	3	6	9	2
9	3	8	6	2	7	5	4	1

3	7	1	8	2	5	4	6	9
6	2	9	3	4	1	5	8	7
4	8	5	7	9	6	3	1	2
1	4	8	9	5	2	6	7	3
7	9	2	4	6	3	8	5	1
5	3	6	1	8	7	9	2	4
8	6	3	2	7	9	1	4	5
9	5	7	6	1	4	2	3	8
2	1	4	5	3	8	7	9	6

7	1	6	3	4	8	9	2	5
9	5	8	6	7	2	1	3	4
3	2	4	9	5	1	7	6	8
6	3	7	2	9	4	8	5	1
1	9	2	8	6	5	4	7	3
4	8	5	7	1	3	6	9	2
8	4	9	5	2	6	3	1	7
5	7	3	1	8	9	2	4	6
2	6	1	4	3	7	5	8	9

Imprint

First Englisch Edition, February 2025
Copyright © 2025 Ariana Naebrich

All rights reserved

Reproduction, even in part, is prohibited. The work, including its parts, is protected by copyright. Any use is prohibited without the consent of the publisher and the author. This applies particularly to electronic or other forms of reproduction, translation, distribution, and public availability.

The pseudonym Ariana Naebrich is represented by: Matthias Kupka, c/o IP-Management #47599, Ludwig-Erhard-Str. 18, 20459 Hamburg, Germany

Manufacturer and Publisher: Independently Published

1st Edition

ISBN: 9798306860503

Made in the USA
Middletown, DE
05 March 2025